MORE PRAISE FOR
Academic Writing as if Readers Matter

"From its title to its final sentence, I loved *Academic Writing as if Readers Matter*. Leonard Cassuto has created a small guidebook packed with big ideas that will help all writers—including natural and social scientists—reach broader audiences by clarifying their message. I plan to reread it periodically."
—Christopher Chabris, *New York Times* bestselling coauthor of
   The Invisible Gorilla: How Our Intuitions Deceive Us

"Brimming with invaluable advice and practical tips, this handbook should be read by any academic who wants *their* book to be read."
—Kevin M. Kruse, Princeton University

"Elegant, eloquent, useful, and necessary, this book is an exemplary act of intellectual citizenship at a time when it's more imperative than ever before to get across to the public what academics do and why it's valuable. (This means you, dear professor.)"
—Rick Perlstein, *New York Times* bestselling author of
   Nixonland: The Rise of a President and the Fracturing of America

"This witty and generous book offers a treasury of sound advice, astute analysis, and clear examples of dos and don'ts. Cassuto shows what it takes to welcome readers rather than alienate them."
—Andrew Delbanco, author of *College: What It Was, Is, and
   Should Be*

"*Academic Writing as if Readers Matter* will make almost anyone a better writer (it's already having that effect on me), and that makes it a very rare and valuable thing. Professors and students need to read this book."
—Carlo Rotella, author of *The World Is Always Coming to an End*

"With charm and wit, Cassuto argues that successful academic writing is an act of generosity toward the reader. He provides concrete strategies to help any scholar or student write in a way that genuinely engages readers."
—Rachael Cayley, author of *Thriving as a Graduate Writer*

Academic
Writing
as if
Readers
Matter

SKILLS FOR SCHOLARS

Academic Writing as if Readers Matter

Leonard Cassuto

PRINCETON UNIVERSITY PRESS
Princeton & Oxford

Published by Princeton University Press
41 William Street, Princeton, New Jersey 08540
99 Banbury Road, Oxford OX2 6JX

press.princeton.edu

Library of Congress Cataloging-in-Publication Data

Names: Cassuto, Leonard, 1960– author.
Title: Academic writing as if readers matter / Leonard Cassuto.
Description: Princeton, New Jersey : Princeton University Press, 2024. |
    Series: Skills for scholars | Includes bibliographical references and index.
Identifiers: LCCN 2024005094 (print) | LCCN 2024005095 (ebook) |
    ISBN 9780691263601 (hardback) | ISBN 9780691195797 (paperback) |
    ISBN 9780691256610 (ebook)
Subjects: LCSH: Academic writing. | Authors and readers. | BISAC:
    LANGUAGE ARTS & DISCIPLINES / Writing / Academic & Scholarly |
    EDUCATION / Schools / Levels / Higher
Classification: LCC LB2369 .C354 2024 (print) | LCC LB2369 (ebook) |
    DDC 808.02—dc23/eng/20240308
LC record available at https://lccn.loc.gov/2024005094
LC ebook record available at https://lccn.loc.gov/2024005095

British Library Cataloging-in-Publication Data is available

Editorial: Matt Rohal and Alena Chekanov
Production Editorial: Natalie Baan
Text and Cover Design: Heather Hansen
Production: Erin Suydam
Publicity: Alyssa Sanford and Kathryn Stevens
Copyeditor: Katherine Harper

This book has been composed in FreightText and FreightSans with Family

Printed in the United States of America

10 9 8 7 6 5 4 3 2 1

For my mother, Thalia Cassuto

Contents

Academic
Writing
as if
Readers
Matter

Introduction

The Primal Scene of Academic Writing

All academic writers begin their journeys in the classroom. There they write for an audience of one person: the teacher.

Professors read students' work as evaluators. The evaluator has a specific job: to read their students' writing from beginning to end and assess it. (The job usually includes writing a response, too, but let's put that task aside.)

The central quality of the evaluator's job is thoroughness. She will read your work closely and completely. One of my former teachers, Edward Tayler, described it this way:

> With proper allowance for human weakness, you may reasonably hope for an attentive, sympathetic reading of every word you write—a kind of reading you may not reasonably hope for ever again.[1]

This kind of careful reading is a gift. As Simone Weil put it: "Attention is the rarest and purest form of generosity."[2]

But there's another concrete and essential reason why student writers may expect this careful attention: *the reader is getting paid*.

The evaluator's position as a paid reader is the exact opposite of the general reader's. General readers pay for the privilege of reading (by buying books or magazines, or subscribing to websites), and they feel no obligation whatever to be thorough. General readers will quit reading if they don't enjoy what they're doing, or if they don't feel they're getting something worthwhile out of the experience.

Every academic writer begins by writing for a captive audience: someone who is literally being paid to pay attention. Long before they set foot in graduate school or venture beyond it, academic writers spend years getting used to a reader who can't be distracted or discouraged, because that reader receives cash to read to the end.[3]

The main problem with writing for a captive audience is that it teaches us to take the reader's attention for granted. Student writers learn to be long-winded because they know—consciously or not—that their reader won't quit on them. They can begin a mile away from their topic and slowly work their way in. Or they may supply three examples where one will do (usually to fill up pages to reach an assigned word limit—tell me you've never done that), all because they trust that the reader will dutifully trudge through.

When student writers sit down to write for a paid audience of one, they enact the primal scene of academic writing. Like other mythical moments of originary consciousness—the fall of Adam and Eve, the Freudian discovery of civilization's discontents, and so on—this primal scene portends disappointment. It points to its own future failures.

But academic writing's primal scene begets far worse than prolixity. Its worst symptom is that it promotes a disconnection from, and disregard for, the reader.

If you know that your readers will stay with you no matter what, you don't have to worry too much about how you treat them. Instead of working to care for the reader, academic writers are taught by their earliest experience that readers are unconditionally invested. They require no consideration because they're already on the hook. That unfortunate lesson invites all kinds of bad writing, and with it the genesis of this book.

Like all primal scenes, the academic writer's beginning ripples forward to affect the future. Academic writers don't leave our primal scene behind. Instead, we re-create and repeat it. (I know I have. I've made many of the mistakes that I warn against in this book.) After we pass the stage of writing for an audience of one, we go on to make many of the same bad moves when we write for wider audiences, often with the hope of getting published. Unexamined bad habits become enshrined. Care for the reader remains an afterthought—or no thought at all.

The primal scene thus stays with us ever after. Writing a paper for your undergraduate professor, a dissertation for a committee, and an article for publication are really three versions of the same exercise, separated by time and experience. Like the professor who reads a student's work, the evaluators of journal and book submissions are paid readers also.*

I'll have more to say presently about how to create a more generous relation between the academic writer and the academic reader—a lot more. I'll also give unvarnished advice about other writing matters.

In a book full of rules and principles, here's the first one:

Even if the reader is being paid, it is better to write as though he or she were not. Write to earn your reader's attention, and then keep on earning it.

On Rules (and Rule-Breaking)

I wrote this book for two main reasons. The first is that academic writing has a bad public reputation, with painful results that affect us all. Imagine standing up to announce that most scholarly books and articles are boring, impenetrable, or worse. The response

---

* Wait, I hear you say: article evaluators typically aren't paid. That's technically true (though the readers of submitted book manuscripts usually are compensated). But evaluators who teach at colleges and universities are paid for what is ambiguously called "service," a category that includes this kind of work. There's also an implied quid pro quo that promotes focused attention: I read the work of my peers with care so that they will do the same for me. Whether through the influence of pay or barter, the author of a scholarly submission may expect a careful and complete reading just as the student author of a seminar paper does.

would be a collective shrug—because that sentiment has become a virtual cliché. Most academic writing is assumed to be bad. Every academic writer starts out in that deep hole.

I would characterize the problem differently. I find that most academic writing is unfriendly and ungenerous. Too many academic writers treat their readers indifferently, or worse. But our readers are the reason that academia—and academic writing— exist in the first place. Poor academic writing contributes to a larger lack of respect for academic work.

That disrespect is everybody's business. If higher education is a public good—and it must be—then it must interact fruitfully with the wider public. Yet the writers working in higher education mistreat various publics, including our closest community of fellow academic readers. Too much academic writing sends an unfortunate message to readers: you don't matter.

Every academic writer—whether student or teacher— represents all the others. Yes, each writer is a free agent. But academic writers also take part in a shared system of inquiry. We matter to each other—and to our readers—as a group. As I will suggest, that's why we must write well: because our work matters to more than just ourselves.

Which brings me to my second reason for this book: because reading most academic writing is work. I mean that in both the literal and the figurative sense. Reading academic writing is literally part of many people's jobs. Figuratively, doing that job can be a slog—it's work to get through the stuff. We (and by "we," I don't mean just professors and students, but anyone engaged in serious intellectual inquiry) may read academic writing as part of our jobs, but that doesn't mean that reading it has to feel like work. Put simply, most academic writing is reader-*unfriendly*.

This unfriendliness problem also affects all of us—and again, I don't mean only people who work at colleges and universities. Academic writing, like the intellectual mission it demonstrates, badly needs renovation, lest it be dismissed and torn down by a public that is increasingly skeptical about it. The public judges us by what we say, starting with how we say it. I hope that this book will help individual writers. I hope, too, that it will lead to writing that helps readers. And, finally, I hope that it will also aid the larger effort to reinforce the frayed relations between town and gown.

What about AI?

As I was finishing this book, artificial intelligence (AI) abruptly arose as a frightening specter on the writing landscape. Language Learning Models such as ChatGPT are already provoking questions of whether writing will soon turn into the esoteric practice of a small population of specialists. The role of Generative AI will surely shake out in the coming years, and I offer my own early thoughts on that subject in the appendix to this book. The capacities of AI already amaze—but they don't include conscious, connected communication.

The idea of writing as communication lies at the center of this book. A writer who does a good job forges a connection with the reader, and sympathetic understanding flows back and forth. Too much academic writing lacks writerly effort to create that connection. Nor is the problem limited to academic writing. Today's public sphere is filled with too much noise and not enough actual communication.

If academics are to fulfill their role as teachers, then we ought to model communication—a connection between writer and reader—at every level of the academic enterprise. AI can't do that because it lacks sensibility. This must be the job of actual human writers. Any writing that goes beyond "souped-up auto-correct" (as economist Paul Krugman has described AI) requires that the writer seek understanding and connection with other humans.[4] How to connect is a skill that's not limited to writing—but writing can teach it. And we can use more of it in the world.

All of this brings me to . . . cooking. Perhaps you've read the magazine *Cook's Illustrated*. The format of a typical *CI* article is: "I set out to make the perfect version of a potato gratin." The writer will then continue: "I was looking for that perfect combination of crisp potato crust and mealy interior, the just-right balance of cream and cheesy tang in the sauce. So I cooked 192 versions of the dish in which I fiddled with all the variables (ingredients, temperatures, cooking times, and so forth) until I got each element just right. Let me describe what I did. And finally, let me present the perfect recipe for a potato gratin."

That's how *CI* founding editor Christopher Kimball and his epigones cook. You may say that you have your recipe for a dish and I have mine, and to each their own taste. Not Kimball. He'll inform you with conviction that his recipe is the right one. You might say he's a fascist cook, but after trying some of his recipes, I can say that his flavors run on time.*

There's a value to knowing a set of rules. Rules put the struts under the wings of imagination. If you learn the rules that govern a cuisine, you'll know how to invent a recipe within that cuisine or experiment outside of it. If you learn the rules that govern writing, you can be creative within any set of conventions. *Of course you can—and sometimes should!—break those rules, but not before you show that you know them.* Otherwise, you will, in the words of one of my old teachers, be presumed to have made a mistake rather than a point.[5]

For Example

Jazz musicians knew that soulfulness and spontaneity are the product of discipline and responsibility.   **—LOUIS MENAND**

---

* In 2015 Kimball was forced out of the magazine he founded after more than twenty years, but *Cook's Illustrated* continues undaunted. So does Kimball, who has started a new venture, *Milk Street*. I mention these things not just because I like to cook tasty food but also because I want to illustrate the proper function of a footnote, which should act something like an extended parenthesis. More on footnotes in chapter 3.

But what about the danger that rules can restrict and exclude? In a 2015 review of Umberto Eco's *How to Write a Thesis*, literary critic Hua Hsu talked about the relevance of rules to scholarly conversation. The "protocols and standards" that feature in research and writing guides like Eco's (and also the one you're reading), says Hsu, "offer a vision of our best selves." Hsu channels Eco's belief that following these rules "allows the average person entry into a veritable universe of argument and discussion."

A common criticism of rulebooks these days is that they exclude members of disadvantaged groups. Many members of these groups are first-generation entrants to colleges, universities, and other intellectual collectives. The concern is that too many rules oppose the learning needs of an increasingly diverse community of scholars. Much good pedagogy is directed at meeting such students "where they are." I try to do that in my own classrooms.

But rules need not discourage community or isolate its would-be members. Rules can also build communities. They can bring readers and writers together. Hsu suggests that the changing demographics of the academy make Eco's call for rules all the more vital, because rules ensure clarity and unity within an ever more diverse conversation. The more voices engaged, the more valuable the rules of engagement.[6]

This book presents a lot of rules, so before I go further, I want to make my rationale clear.

The first and most important test of a writing rule is whether it produces good writing. But "good writing" is a subjective term, you may say. That's true, so let's keep it simple: good writing is writing that meets the needs of its audience. These needs will, of course, differ by case. The reader of a user's manual for a television set and the reader of a scholarly history of the Balkans aren't seeking the same experience. I'll address the specific needs of the academic reader in chapter 1.

Consider the vexing case of the first-person pronoun. Most writers have been taught never to say "I" in their expository writing. Judging from what my students tell me, the ban has invariably been presented as a rule with no explanation other than "because it's not proper," which is really no explanation at all. ***The blanket rule against "I" is a bad rule*** because it produces bad results. Lots of serious writing benefits when the writer steps forward. You're the one doing the talking, after all, not an anonymous and impersonal voice intoning, "It is interesting to note that."

Of course, certain kinds of writing may benefit when you don't say "I." In much lab science writing, the procedure matters more than the person carrying it out, so it can be useful to efface the experimenter to highlight the experiment. But my point is that the absolute prohibition of the first-person pronoun reflects unexamined dogmatism rather than a concern for good writing. Good rules must come with good reasons.

Tip
Don't avoid contractions.

The rule against contractions is another bad one. True, contractions tend to be informal and academic writing tends toward the formal, but it's also valuable to sound like a person, not a stuffed shirt. Moreover, contractions often provide the smoothest passage through a sentence. If I had used "it is" instead of "it's" earlier in this paragraph, it wouldn't have sounded right to me.

You needn't use contractions as often as I do, but you shouldn't avoid them just because someone warned you against them. The proof lies in the result.

When you lay down rules, you also have to allow for changes—and that's another reason to know the "why" behind the rule. I'll supply reasons in this book, and I'll acknowledge changes. Language evolves. Here are a few quick examples. The word "nauseous" originally meant "causing nausea" (as in, "The smell of that sour milk is nauseous"). But the word's usage has changed over time. Now it also means "nauseated"—that is, about to vomit ("That sour milk made me nauseous"). In fact, the "nauseated" definition has largely displaced the older meaning of "causing nausea." Likewise, "data" used to be a plural noun (with "datum" as the singular). Now it's mostly used in the singular, a usage I follow here. The word "hopefully" used to mean "with hope" ("'May I have a cookie?' she asked hopefully"). Now it also means "it is to be hoped" ("Hopefully the cookie jar has been left unattended"). In this case, too, the newer definition has elbowed the older one aside.

I don't love all these changes, but I accept them. (Well, most of them. I choose to use "hopefully" only the old way.) Personal pronoun usage is undergoing rapid change right now, so rapid that I won't suggest any rules to govern pronouns in this book. At the time of this writing, the singular *they* is being used by the *New York Times*, but the *Chicago Manual of Style* approves of it only in "informal" writing.

Like all writers, I prefer certain changes over others, but I try to stay open to possibility. That is, I don't fancy myself a "prescriptive grammarian" in all ways. I want rules only when they make sense.

Perhaps, then, I'm not quite the dictator that Christopher Kimball is when he enters the kitchen. Surely there's more than one way to cook something. The proof, you might say, is in the pudding. Moreover, tastes change. Yet Kimball's chocolate chip cookie is pretty damned good. If you want to depart from the established standard, you should have a reason.[7]

The usage of the word "unique" shows the need for rules. The word means "one of a kind," and therefore it accepts no comparisons. One thing cannot be "more unique" than another. That's a good rule, and I correct writers when they break it, because "somewhat unique" has no meaning, and "relatively unique" is like saying "sort of pregnant."

While I'm wearing my grammarian's hat, I will offer the Grammarian's Most Important Rule: ***Don't look like an idiot if you can avoid it***. You can qualify "unique" in a small number of sensible ways ("nearly unique" is okay, for instance, because it's logical). Stray from those and you'll find that it's not a good look—and a bad look hurts your credibility, and with it your writerly fortunes.

I have focused so far on the smallest possible examples—single words—but rules likewise apply to sentences, paragraphs, and whole arguments. Usage, like scholarship, changes "by methodological consent"—which is to say, gradually.[8] I'll work through the rules from the large to the small in this book. After an opening chapter on the special needs of the academic reader, I'll present some rules in chapter 2 for the construction of arguments, paragraphs, and sentences. Chapter 3 will look at words, with a particular focus on jargon. Chapter 4 concludes the book with an argument that academic writing must change—for the sake of academics and academic work, and for the sake of readers. All of this guidance points toward an overarching goal: We need to value and respect our audiences better.

If you want to bestow that respect on your reader, then one priority should prevail: clarity. Writers make decisions all the time. How long should this sentence be? How much detail should I go into to explain a concept? Should the ending look back toward what I have already done or forward to the new ideas I've brought into view? The answers are judgment calls, shaped by experience—and rules.

The answers also arise from practical common sense: what will work best. Should I use the first person? Should I tell an illustrative story? Should I start with a scene or a thesis statement? The overarching question that governs all of these cases and many others is, "Will doing this help me make my point clearly, and in a way likely to grab and keep my reader's attention?"

As the writer, you are the first judge of your work. The basis for your judgment should be what is clearest and, more broadly, what will best meet the reader's needs.

In the end, it comes down to that. We make judgment calls to persuade the reader, so the reader is our second judge. Groups of readers make up audiences—and I'll be considering how to address more- and less-specialized audiences in the second half of this book. But it all starts with the relation between writer and reader. If we make moves that make us less persuasive to the reader, those moves must be mistakes. The most important rule is to avoid mistakes, and this book will help you do that.

But don't be afraid to break the rules—if it advances your cause.

The best sentence I've ever seen breaks lots of them. The following extract is from Martin Luther King, Jr.'s 1963 "Letter from Birmingham Jail." In the second sentence, King's rage against "white moderates" takes the form of a slow burn:

> I guess it is easy for those who have never felt the stinging darts of segregation to say "wait." But when you have seen vicious mobs lynch your mothers and fathers at will and drown your sisters and brothers at whim; when you have seen hate-filled policemen curse, kick, brutalize, and even kill your black brothers and sisters with impunity; when you see the vast majority of your twenty million Negro brothers smothering in an airtight cage of poverty in the midst of an affluent society; when you suddenly find your tongue twisted and your speech stammering as you seek to explain to your six-year-old daughter why she cannot go to the public amusement park that has just been advertised on television, and see tears welling up in her little eyes when she is told that Funtown is closed to colored children, and see the depressing clouds of inferiority begin to form in her little mental sky, and see her begin to distort her little personality by unconsciously developing a bitterness toward white people; when you have to concoct an answer for a five-year-old son asking in agonizing pathos, "Daddy, why do white people treat colored people so mean?"; when you take a cross-country drive and find it necessary to sleep night after night in the uncomfortable corners of your

automobile because no motel will accept you; when you are humiliated day in and day out by nagging signs reading "white" and "colored"; when your first name becomes "nigger" and your middle name becomes "boy" (however old you are) and your last name becomes "John," and when your wife and mother are never given the respected title "Mrs."; when you are harried by day and haunted by night by the fact that you are a Negro, living constantly at tiptoe stance, never knowing what to expect next, and plagued with inner fears and outer resentments; when you are forever fighting a degenerating sense of "nobodyness"—then you will understand why we find it difficult to wait.

You might say that King's sentence runs on. (It's 318 words long.) I think you would also say that it works. And it works precisely *because* it runs on, because its long windup creates pressure that parallels the pressure that King is writing about.

Try This

Practice creative rule-breaking. You can only do so if you already know the rules. Be thankful someone bothered to teach you these rules, or be angry that no one felt it was worth the trouble to teach you—angry enough that you go off and learn them yourself.   **—MIN HYOUNG SONG**

Furthermore

There is no moral or ethical reason to spell a word in the way that intelligent readers expect to see it spelled. But if you don't spell the word in the conventional way, intelligent readers will assume that you are merely ignorant, and they will be right.

—EDWARD MENDELSON

On the other hand, here's a case where breaking the rules does *not* make sense: on a *curriculum vitae* (cv), or academic résumé. Readers of cv's have definite habits. When you write yours, you should typically lead with your school credentials, because cv readers (including potential employers and grant and scholarship givers) almost always look for that information right away. It does not behoove you to annoy them by burying it.

Similarly, when you lay out your cv, you should follow the conventions of your discipline. If scientists expect your publications to be presented in chronological order and in a specific bibliographic format, then why not meet their expectations? If you don't, you'll distract them from their most important task, which is to assess your credentials. A cv is not the place to challenge your reader's assumptions or expectations. It's an arena where you should typically follow the rules.

Rules help because they ease communication. Breaking them makes sense when the exceptions ease communication. So learn the rules—and after you do, be alert to where they may not apply. If you want to be persuasive, *flout convention when you need to, but only if you can show your reader—at the same time—that you know what you're doing.* Be chatty in an academic essay, write in the second person, quote Wikipedia, mix footnotes and endnotes, or add a surprise ending—as long as it makes you understandable and convincing to your reader. Sometimes it will. But let's be realistic here: you won't want to make these risky moves very often.

One rule supersedes all the others: **You can do anything as long as it works.**

How to Read This Book

You should read this book any way you want. At one point while writing it, I was calling it *How to Take Care of the Academic Reader.* You're the reader, and I want to take care of you, not order you around. My central point is that good academic writing depends on that care—which most academic writers don't learn how to give. For that reason, I devote chapter 1 to that idea alone. There, I explain the relation between academic writer and academic reader in a series of metaphors. (In the process, I make a case for the use of metaphor in academic writing—and for having some fun where and when you can.)

Then come the rules, advice, and tips on how to make good academic arguments in good academic prose. (The rules and tips appear in *italic* or **boldface** type, the most important ones in ***both***.) The two middle chapters form a sequence that starts globally and gradually works down to the local details: Chapter 2 focuses on the argument, first on the whole and then its parts: introductions and conclusions, transitions, signposts, paragraphs, sentences. Chapter 3 centers on words and phrases, with a spotlight on the use and misuse of jargon. The final chapter, "Why We Must," moves outward again. There, I discuss what is at stake for all of us, and why good academic writing ought to matter to all academic writers, separately and together.

In other words, this book is a sandwich. The hefty helping of tips and techniques is the filling. Surrounding the filling and holding it all together is my larger argument about why the link between academic writer and reader is so important.

No one should tell you how to eat a sandwich, and I'm not going to try. You can skip right to the specifics in the middle if you want—I won't be offended. Please read this book however you like; I'm grateful that you're reading it at all. But that first chapter is there because the later specifics balance atop its foundational idea that good academic writing is about a relationship, a connection with your reader. And the first step is to look more closely at that reader.

The Care and Feeding of the Academic Reader

When I write, it's to connect.
I have a total responsibility to the reader. The reader has to trust me and never feel betrayed.

—PETER SCHJELDAHL[1]

Relationship Advice: The Clasp of the Hand

As a writer, you enter into a relationship with your reader. You're someone with information who wants (and maybe needs) to share it, and your reader is someone who wants (and maybe needs) information. Another way to put this: you are different from your audience, but each of you seeks something from the other.

Here's the guiding message of this book: *Care for your reader.* Create a friendly and generous relationship with your audience.

Here's the central metaphor in this book: imagine your relationship with your reader as you reaching out and clasping your reader's hand.

The handclasp describes a meeting of two minds. More important, it captures the idea of care. You need to create a mutual relationship with your audience in which you seek to understand each other. In this process, you try to comprehend the needs of your audience, while your audience tries to comprehend your argument.

All writers have to figure out what their readers do and don't know. It doesn't make sense to lecture a professional tennis player on how many points it takes to win a tiebreaker, any more than you would need to remind a European historian that the Treaty of Westphalia broke the power of the Holy Roman Empire.

But it's dangerous to assume too much background for your reader. Because scholarly writing centers on the idea of expertise, this pitfall is ever-present. For graduate students, who are seeking certification as experts, it's a constant danger. ***Be a generous expert.***

Let me put it another way: many graduate student writers are afraid of appearing to talk down to specialist readers who have more experience than they do. The inexperienced writer fears that these experienced readers will think the writer believes them to be simpletons, and so the writer skips "unnecessary" background.

That's a misplaced fear, because even specialists don't mind being oriented. When academic writers (including a disproportionate number of dissertation writers) skip over the basics, they lose a chance to introduce themselves and show the reader where their ideas come from. That lack of background produces pernicious results.

As the writer, you're creating a place for the reader to inhabit. It should be one that the reader is happy to occupy. When you explain stuff the reader may already know, you show how you understand this shared knowledge by how you teach it. Imagine you're writing about the bluesman Muddy Waters. You might say, in effect, I'm a blues fan, and I see Waters in a certain way. Insiders—aficionados of blues, and also of gospel and soul—will appreciate knowing where you're coming from, and they'll learn more about your point of view by watching you cogently explain something they already know to readers who lack that background.

When a writer omits these explanations out of concern that the reader will be bored (or worse, offended because she already knows it), the reader never gets comfortably situated. A few years ago, I read a graduate student's description of Kurt Vonnegut's "famous attempt to write an 'anti-glacier' book." In fact, the reference is not famous, or even known outside of microspecialist niches. I certainly had never heard of it before my student brought it up.

From this unexplained reference, a reader might infer that the writer won't deign to address a lightweight who doesn't know this "famous" commonplace. That brushoff would encompass approximately 99 percent of scholarly readers, to say nothing of nonscholars. No writer wants to alienate that much of their readership, obviously. But that's what happens when you don't think clearly about the needs of your audience.

Youthful anxiety may create the need to talk down to the audience—to prove that you know stuff. That's a mistake, and it can persist long after dark hair turns white. Wielding expertise like a cudgel is a skill that academic writers may refine over time, witnessed in these two examples from the work of senior scholars:

> As everyone is aware, development today is a field of action in a "new regime of unequal international relations."[2]

By now we are all familiar with discussions of "unexpressed language," neatly codified in recent years as a sociolinguistic phenomena [*sic*].[3]

The writers' declarations that "Everyone is aware" or "We are all familiar with" translate to "Surely you must know." Well, what if I don't? Scorn likely won't motivate me to find out. **Please don't be mean to the reader**, whose only sin is the desire to learn things.

Academic writers are teachers. Most academics learn to teach in classrooms while in graduate school, but I'm not talking only about that specific activity. *Academic writing is also teaching*: you are teaching your research to someone else.

When we talk about teaching, we should talk about learning. What you intend to teach with your writing matters less than what your readers take from it. You may write for specialists or for wider audiences, but either way, you need to think about the needs of your readers. That Vonnegut reference implies that the reader is an expert already. It's as though you're trying to teach someone to drive, but instead of starting with a typical automatic-transmission car, you begin with a motorcycle with manual transmission, no pedals, and the clutch mounted on the handlebar. Don't assume that the reader can just climb aboard one of those and zoom off alongside you.

Bad scholarly writers reside too deep inside their own heads and not enough in the reader's. If you invoke the theorist Fredric Jameson's idea of a "postmodern hyperspace" without explaining it, then no one who hasn't read a particular work by Jameson can know what this abstraction means. If you proceed without supplying that explanation, you pull away from the curb with only Jameson's careful readers as your passengers. An unfamiliar reader may get a sense of what you're talking about, but her comprehension will be limited. So you see what's at stake if you don't forge the understanding you need. As a writer, you will lose a large portion of your potential readership.

Many well-known scholars don't teach their work very well to outside readers. They might be excellent classroom teachers, but they forget that their teaching extends to their writing, too. They're smart characters, but they don't pay much attention to the needs of their readers. That doesn't mean that you shouldn't continue to enjoy and learn from these intellectuals. Just don't try to write like them. Because if you succeed, you will also succeed in confusing and pushing away your reader—which is the opposite of clasping the reader's hand.

Let me state plainly:

Bad writing disrespects the reader. Fundamentally, that's what makes it bad. You and your reader are in a relationship with each other. How long will anyone want to stay in a relationship with someone who disrespects them?

Bad writing is unfriendly. If good writing clasps the reader's hand, then bad writing leaves the reader abandoned with hand extended.

Bad writing is ungenerous. If the reader gives you her time and attention, you need to offer your own, in the form of writing that makes an effort to understand what the reader is looking for and what she brings to the search.

If you're going to treat your readers respectfully and generously, you need to know as much as you can about how to meet their needs.

On Extended Metaphors

The clasp of the hand is an extended metaphor. ***Maybe you think of extended metaphors as too much like "creative writing" to use in "academic writing." If you've acquired that belief, please discard it.*** Now stretch your limbs and feel the new freedom of movement you have. Then recall the first principle of reverse engineering, which is to work backward from what works. If extended metaphors can help you reach your goal, then it's the right choice to use them.

How can a tool be "too creative" to use, anyway? Creative writing is—by definition—original in some way. If something isn't original, then it can't be called creative. A more accurate label in that case may be "clichéd." Clichés belong to everybody. It's worth the effort to make something of your own.

Metaphors are part of how we think, not ornaments that decorate our completed thoughts. Linguists George Lakoff and Mark Johnson say that "human thought processes are largely metaphorical."[4] I use a lot of metaphors in this book because they offer a chance for an "aha!" moment of understanding. Also, they're fun.

Better inventors of metaphors have shown me how they can bring joy. In September 1902, Wilbur Wright, the elder of the Wright Brothers, devised a metaphor to begin perhaps the most important public appearance of his life. Wright's address to the Western Society of Engineers about the gliding experiments he had been conducting with his brother Orville was his first public speech. He gave the speech an understated title: "Some Aeronautical Experiments." A Wright Brothers biographer later described it as "The Book of Genesis of the twentieth-century Bible of Aeronautics."[5] It's one of the most important works of science writing ever.

Much of Wright's speech, which was widely reprinted afterward, is understandably technical. But before he descended into the mathematics of his work with his brother, he described that work with a striking analogy. The Wright Brothers designed their flying machine based on their observations of birds aloft. How do birds balance on the wind? Wright illustrated the question by dropping a piece of paper from his hand:

If I take this piece of paper, and after placing it parallel with the ground, quickly let it fall, it will not settle steadily down as a staid, sensible piece of paper ought to do, but it insists on contravening every recognized rule of decorum, turning over and darting hither and thither in the most erratic manner, much after the style of an untrained horse.[6]

Wright compares the paper to a bird in order to show that riding the wind is harder than it may look. Then he compares the bird to a horse for the purpose of trying to domesticate its flight. To tame "a fractious horse," Wright said, you have to mount it and "learn by actual practice how each motion and trick may be best met." That's why the Wrights decided "to mount a machine" to fly.

Wright's use of the falling paper as a metaphor for the problem of flight is particularly vivid. He presents a literal picture—and by so doing, shows how metaphors generate images that teach.

Wright's comparisons prove that you don't have to be a poet to use a metaphor. Metaphors persuade: they have helped to win many an election. (Some quick examples: the New Deal, Morning in America, A thousand points of light.) Metaphors teach—and that's what academic writers especially seek to do. They're quick-acting and powerful images that distill the essence of an idea. And metaphors give pleasure—something that writers ought to think about doing whenever they can.

The vividness of metaphors is what makes them such useful writing tools. This extended metaphor underscores the harmony that the author, mathematician Steven Strogatz, is arguing exists in nature:

At the heart of the universe is a steady, insistent beat: the sound of cycles in sync. It pervades nature at every scale from the nucleus to the cosmos. Every night along the tidal rivers of Malaysia, thousands of fireflies congregate in the mangroves and flash in unison, without any leader or cue from the environment. Trillions of electrons march in lockstep in a superconductor, enabling electricity to flow through it with zero resistance. In the solar system, gravitational synchrony can eject huge boulders out of the asteroid belt and toward Earth; the cataclysmic impact of one such meteor is thought to have killed the dinosaurs. Even our bodies are symphonies of rhythm, kept alive by the relentless, coordinated firing of thousands of pacemaker cells in our hearts. In every case, these feats of synchrony occur spontaneously, almost as if nature has an eerie yearning for order.[7]

The brightness and vitality of metaphors spotlight what's going on. In this case, the unity of the metaphor actually helps to link the phenomena that the author invokes. By rendering one thing in terms of another, metaphors ask the audience to create meaning— and to understand.

Metaphors improve your reader's experience. They help the reader to understand you better and enjoy your writing more. For that reason alone, you should use them—and because your reader will get those benefits.

> **Tip**
> *Don't overdose on metaphors.*
>
> When it comes to metaphors, Mae West is wrong: too much of a good thing is *not* wonderful. Metaphors can be wonderfully illustrative tools, but if you let them rain down, you'll tire your readers without enlightening them. Use metaphors; don't overuse them.
>
> Where lies the line between use and overuse? Like most writing decisions, this is a judgment call. Experiment, and assess the results.

In that spirit, this chapter unfolds in the form of three extended metaphors. The clasp of the hand was the first one. The next, a travel metaphor, will show what it means to treat the reader with thoughtful respect. Finally, with a third metaphor I'll turn to the very important specific case of the academic reader, a creature whose particular behavior the academic writer needs to understand.

Writing as a Journey for Two

Emily Dickinson's famous poem "Because I could not stop for Death" imagines the final passage as a ride in Death's carriage, past a school and fields of grain, stopping at the grave itself.[8] In its portrayal of dying as a journey toward eternity in an actual vehicle, the poem turns on an extended metaphor.

Writing is like dying that way (though not in other ways, I hasten to add). I like to think that good writing leads to a good life. But writing can also be rendered as a journey with a driver and a passenger.

An Annotated Extended Metaphor for What Writers Do

—The Metaphor

—The Annotations

1

Imagine that you are offering the reader a journey in your chariot. She accepts your invitation and climbs in next to you. She closes the passenger door, *but she doesn't lock it*. And you're off.

The essential point here is that the writer enters into a voluntary partnership with the reader. That's the nature of writing for an audience. That partnership lasts for the time that the reader spends reading—but of course the writer has to prepare for it beforehand. I'll have more to say about this partnership later on, especially the writerly behavior that ought to govern it.

a. The ride begins with an agreement. Your goal is to transport your passenger to an endpoint that you've got in mind. (Maybe you named it, but maybe you didn't.) You've also promised to create interest along the way, because the reader doesn't just want to fall asleep and arrive someplace. She wants a scenic route that will engage her along the way.

The reader doesn't have to know everything up front about what you mean to do. Signposting is often a good idea in academic writing, but if you're writing a piece with many parts, you don't need to flag every move you're going to make beforehand.

b. An important observation to start: your passenger is taking a risk when she starts this journey. She's making you an offer of trust and time. First, she's trusting you to transport her safely and surely. But more important, she's giving you an irreplaceable gift: her time.

Too many academic writers write as though they believe that they're doing the reader a favor, but: 1) Such writing rarely does anybody any favors; and 2) it misses the point. The reader is the one who's doing something for the writer. She's giving the writer something she'll never get back. The writer needs to remember and respect that always.

2

Now that you're moving, the judgment calls begin. Your job to keep the passenger focused on your shared journey from start to finish, or for as long as she needs to accompany you.

If you divide the reader's attention, you forfeit part of it. If you lose the reader's attention, you're going to have a hard time regaining it.

a. First decision: do you want to tell her where you're going, or keep it a surprise? Or do you want to aim for something in between? You could give her a general sense of your direction and overall goal. You could say something about the lay of the land. (Is there a hilly section? Is it muddy?).

Thesis first, or thesis last? Or some combination? Most academic writing is deductive (thesis first) for good reasons that I'll discuss in more detail elsewhere. But how much you want to explain ahead of time is a judgment call based on the needs of the material.

b. Instead of describing the whole route, you could describe the distance to a halfway point where you'll both recalibrate your bearings.

Perhaps you want to argue that ultra-endurance sports (such as twenty-four-hour races through the desert) are the moral equivalent of a Roman circus. To do that, you might begin with the particular (the case of one runner) and pivot to the general (all runners). In that case, you might choose to preview just the first part of your thesis and wait until you're ready for the pivot before you explain what comes next.

c. There's also the *how* of it all. How much do you want to say about how you'll get there? Maybe you're planning an indirect route to avoid traffic.

And then there's methodology. If your methodology is simple, you probably don't need to preview it up front. But if it's complicated—or if it owes something specific to someone else ("and here I will rely on Clifford Geertz's idea of 'thick description'"), then you may need to tip off the reader.

So what should you say? It depends— as judgments will—on externals. Maybe you're traveling through rough terrain. Maybe there will be a lot of twists and turns. In that event, it can be useful to warn the passenger ahead of time, so she can brace herself and not lurch back and forth.

Or maybe it'll be smooth going, including some long straightaways, but with some abrupt shifts in speed. Your rider may want to know about those. Or you might decide that with a good road and light traffic, you don't need to mention any of that—so you flick your reins and your chariot continues on.

Regardless of whether you prepare a surprise ending, you have to stay in control of your material, and you must convey a sense of control to your reader. A writer out of control—flying from point to point without transitions, say—is a chariot skirting a ditch.

3

Now that you're on the road, you need your passenger's confidence. She has already given that to you, but it's not (as the lawyers say) an irrevocable trust. To keep it, you need to be a good driver. What does that mean? Being attentive to the needs of the passenger.

A good writer maintains the reader's confidence by anticipating her needs. You may know that your argument will go back and forth for a reason, but you might choose to flag it beforehand. ("Poindexter's position may seem redundant, but it's crucial because . . .") One of the reasons that Plato's Republic *is still assigned—besides its profundity—is because of the way that Plato structures the Socratic dialogues to anticipate the reader's possible questions.*

If you don't pay attention what you need to do in order to keep your reader's attention, then why bother writing at all?*

a. You may be following a series of switchbacks, for example, but if your passenger thinks you're just going in circles, she'll stop trusting you. She may start to worry. If she does, she'll spend time and attention wondering whether you're lost. That time and attention is your loss, because it would otherwise go to following the trip.

If you shake your reader's confidence, you lose her attention. It's a zero-sum game: any attention that the reader devotes to wondering whether you know what you're doing is attention lost to your argument. The more of your reader's attention you lose, the less chance that your writing will have any effect.

---

* In academic circles, the answer to this question might be "In order to get published." It's true that publication is capital in the academic world, but so is citation. If you don't acknowledge the reader's needs, you won't get cited—and your writing will fall into an abyss of neglect and never be heard from again.

b. Drive carefully. If you take the turns too sharply, or barrel straight through a stream instead of pausing to look for a bridge, your passenger may further question your judgment, even if you know the water isn't that deep.

Pacing is central, and good pacing requires that you put yourself in your reader's place. You may know where you are, but if your reader thinks you're lost, you might as well be lost—because the reader will get just as rattled as if you actually were. It matters that you know where you're going. But it matters almost as much that the reader believes that you do.

c. If your passenger doesn't like your driving, she may tighten her seat belt and stay put. That would be fortunate for you, but it's still a loss. A suspicious passenger will tense up. She'll focus on your driving and little else, and then she'll be distracted from the trip itself. Loss of trust equals loss of attention. And with her attention divided, your passenger may arrive at the end of the trip with a scant sense of where you've taken her.

If you squander the reader's belief in you, you risk the worst possible outcome: she'll stop reading.

The worst judgment someone can pass on your writing is to want to read it, but then decide not to because it's too hard to follow. You could try blaming that outcome on the reader ("she doesn't understand what I'm trying to do!"), but where does that leave you? Your work still goes unread.

d. Or the worst may happen. The passenger's trust in you may erode, and she may order you to stop so that she can get out. That would be an absolute failure for you as a driver, for the obvious reason that you won't have succeeded in transporting her to the promised destination. When the passenger bails out, the ride—and the journey—end in the middle, unfinished.

4

I stipulated at the start of this story that the passenger side door was unlocked, allowing the passenger to bail out anytime. But what if it were locked, and she couldn't leave until the end of the trip? If she didn't like the way that the trip was going and she couldn't bail out, she would probably quit paying attention. By the time you reached the journey's end, she would be exasperated and fuming at you, the driver.

On the other hand, if your driving maintained the passenger's trust, she might not even notice that the door is locked until you got to the end, when you unlocked it for her to step out.

Academic writing is filled with cases where the reader can't choose to stop reading. If you're a student and a piece of writing is required for a class, you have to read it. If it's necessary background research for something you're writing, you can't skip it.

But a reader who has to push through a piece of writing that she dislikes is not exactly going to become a fan of the writer. More likely, she'll resent the time she had to spend. That reading experience probably won't end well for the writer. More precisely, a reader who dislikes a piece of writing is unlikely to understand it fully, remember it positively, or cite it approvingly, if she cites it at all.

But if you signpost your argument and unfurl it with the reader's needs in mind, you reach for a happy ending in which the reader learns from you and maybe (yes, it's possible!) enjoys the experience. If I sounded a little sarcastic just now, it's because I—like any experienced academic reader—have suffered through my share of bumpy, lurching rides. But I've also sat beside some excellent drivers. Becoming a good writer starts with looking out for the reader. A reader who enjoys reading something is more likely to spread the news about it.

It's now time to look more closely at that reader. The first two metaphors, the clasp of the hand and the secure journey, apply well to many kinds of writing—including academic writing, of course. But the reader of academic writing also has some distinctive peculiarities that academic writers need to notice and attend to.

Why the Academic Reader Is a Different Animal Than the General Reader

This is a book about good academic writing, so it's reasonable to ask what "academic" writing is. After all, much of what makes for good academic writing also makes for good writing, period. That overlap means, I modestly hope, that much of the advice I give in the following pages might be followed by writers of English everywhere.

But there are some important particulars that distinguish academic style from style writ large. Those distinctions arise from who's reading and why. Academic writers must master certain skills and strategies that are particularly appropriate to meet the aims of academic readers. So let's look closely at those readers.

Reading for Use

Scholars form what some of us call a "discourse community." How does this community read?

Literate people read different things in different ways. I read a newspaper differently than I read a novel, and I read a novel that I plan to write about or teach differently than one that I'm reading for pleasure.

With those differences in mind, let me rephrase the question: *How do scholars read when they're actively on the job being scholars?* This question matters because academic writers need to write for those readers. This may sound like a simplistic truism, but it's not, because academic readers have particular needs.* Academic writers should meet those particular needs. When they do, they take care of their readers while they read.

The writer–reader relationship starts with the writer's understanding of what the reader wants and how best to provide it. A writer who thinks in those terms will be less likely to stack long, dense paragraphs atop one another to form eighty-page chapters, for example. And a world with fewer gargantuan chapters will be a better, kinder one in which readers may reach upward toward the light.

"There is a temptation," says literary scholar and historian Andrew Delbanco, "to just write for people who already know a lot about the subject and are going to read whatever you write because they need to, not because it's pleasurable or exciting."[9] Let's focus on the habits of the community that Delbanco identifies. These are people who read things because they need to.

Writing to that group isn't necessarily a "temptation." Many scholars write to their fellow specialists for good reasons. Not every subject of inquiry possesses the potential for general interest, after all. Delbanco, like all researchers, is one of those need-driven readers himself. So is everybody, in fact, from professors to consumers who pore over the user's manual for their new air conditioner.

But there's no denying that scholars are prominent members of the group that Delbanco has identified here. All academics, from art historians to astrophysicists, read a lot of things because we need to. Maybe you're reading this book because you feel that you need to—though I hope you're getting some fun out of it too. Either way, we shouldn't deny that researchers read for reasons of need.

So now we can refine the original question even further: *How do people read when they're reading things because they need to?* Here, finally, is the answer:

---

* Academic writers sometimes need to write for general readers too, but that's a different subject, which I'll take up in chapter 4.

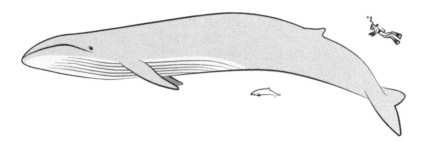

This is a blue whale, a member of the suborder called baleen whales. Baleen whales have no teeth. Instead, their mouths contain hundreds of baleen plates made of keratin, the same substance that forms our fingernails. The plates hang in the whale's mouth like a curtain, and they overlap and interlock to form a giant strainer. A blue whale feeds by taking a giant gulp of water and then using its tongue to force the water out between the plates.

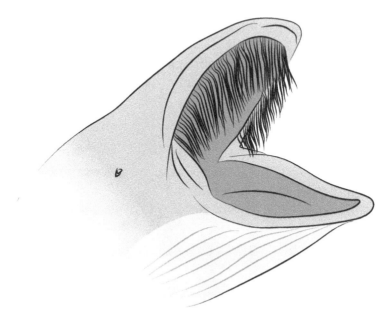

The water exits, and the plates trap tiny crustaceans called krill inside the whale's mouth. The whale swallows these, presumably without tasting them. It then repeats the process again and again, all day long. A blue whale can easily eat around eight thousand pounds of krill a day.

Remember this: **Academic readers are like blue whales**. When researchers read, they take in large amounts of information and strain out what they intend to use in their own work. Like blue whales, academic readers retain only what will benefit them. They don't read casually, but intentionally—it's a kind of work.

General readers usually don't want to work when they read. The general reader may savor a book or article, lingering over the best parts. Or she may race through, wanting to know what happens next. If the academic reader is a blue whale amassing nutrients in quantity, we might imagine the general reader as a discerning cat or an eager dog in a pet food commercial. Whether delicately sampling their food or happily snarfing it up, general readers seek pleasure above all. We know this to be true because we're all general readers in our spare time. When general readers aren't having fun, we'll put down the book or article, pick something else up, or maybe go bowling.

The Feeding of the Academic Reader

So how do you write for a use-driven reader? Here's the first principle: **recognize that blue whales are special animals that require particular treatment.**

Researchers understand the idea of reading for use because we've all done it, starting with our first high school research papers or even earlier. Yet we don't think of our own readers as behaving this way. There's a strange narcissism that persists among academic writers. We recognize that we read other people's writing in order to extract the valuable parts, but we still imagine that they read *our* stuff just because they like to.

This obviously isn't so, but once we recognize that fact, we have to act on it. In other words, we have to consider the behaviors of

For Example

Disciplines have their own presentation conventions that guide academic readers looking for certain kinds of information. Scholarly monographs usually contain a section in the introduction where the writer briefly summarizes each chapter. In the sciences, the journal *Nature* provides its contributors with a pithy description of the conventions for section headings in a scientific article:

- The *Introduction* section clarifies the motivation for the work presented and prepares readers for the structure of the paper.
- The *Materials and Methods* section provides sufficient detail for other scientists to reproduce the experiments presented in the paper. In some journals, this information is placed in an appendix, because it is not what most readers want to know first.
- The *Results* and *Discussion* sections present and discuss the research results, respectively. They are often usefully combined into one section, however, because readers can seldom make sense of results alone without accompanying interpretation—they need to be told what the results mean.
- The *Conclusion* section presents the outcome of the work by interpreting the findings at a higher level of abstraction than the *Discussion* and by relating these findings to the motivation stated in the *Introduction*.

The point of such conventions is to create a shared sense of expectation between writer and use-driven reader.

someone who reads the way a blue whale eats. How does this species behave? What happens when the academic whale encounters a book or article?

It shouldn't prove too hard to figure this out. If you're reading this book, you probably know how to read for use already, so it's a matter of reflecting on your own practice.

Reading for use is easy to explain. First, you figure out whether a source is useful. Sometimes the title will provide a clue, or perhaps you found the work because it was cited in another one that you're using.* Either way, you're going to do a quick assessment to see how deeply you're going to want to read into it. If it's an article, how far are you going to read or skim? If it's a book, are you going to read all of it, or parts? Which parts?[10]

Once you find out which sections of it are useful, you then extract the relevant information. You might lift out data, concepts, examples, or all three. You'll store them in your own files, where they'll be ready for use in your own writing, teaching, or other work. If that all seems simple, that's because at its core, it is. How the writer should act on this information is more complicated.

Writing for Use

Now that we've studied the behavior of the academic reader in nature, we can turn to the writer who provides the reading material. Let's begin with the academic writer's professional goals.

The most important goal centers on audience. In order to impress any audience, you have to persuade. If you're a graduate student working on a paper or a dissertation, you must persuade your professor or adviser of the value of what you're saying. That effort will segue into later attempts to persuade editors and peer reviewers to lift the gate and let you into print.

---

* Or perhaps you were browsing in a library stack and found something that looks interesting shelved next to the book you were seeking. Digital natives, take note: this is another great way to find sources.

Once you're published, your eventual goal is to be noticed by even more readers and to persuade them to give you a signal boost. In the academic world, that boost typically takes the form of citations. Publication means entering the conversation: getting yourself invited to the table. But citation means you're affecting the conversation. There's a distinction between the first goal and the second, and it's again based on reading.

Use-driven readers recognize that not every piece of writing will prove equally useful. Researchers encounter a lot of articles and books when they investigate a topic. They don't read them from beginning to end because that's impossible. Once you realize something isn't useful, you stop reading it. Sometimes you only last a page or two—more about that in a minute.

If you want to be cited, your work has to be sticky (that is, memorable). You have to persuade the reader to keep reading. Or, to put it in the terms I've been using, you have to meet the needs of the reader who would cite you. In other words: ***It's the job of the academic writer to help the reader who is reading for use.*** If that task seems obvious, then ask yourself why so many academic writers fail to perform it.

To help the use-driven reader, a writer has to think like one. That's eminently possible, given that researchers have all worn that hat and know what it feels like. To put yourself in your reader's place is an act of sympathy, or common feeling: you're trying to understand the reader's experience from the inside out. Eighteenth-century "Common Sense" philosophers such as Adam Smith and David Hume tried hard to figure out exactly how sympathy worked, but we don't have to get into those particulars here.* For now, let's just focus on the main ingredient of a sympathetic bond with the reader: the ability to imagine what the reader wants and needs.

---

* We now understand the phrase "common sense" to mean something obvious ("duh"), but its original meaning pointed to feelings that could be shared among people—and the Greek root of the word "sympathy" literally describes that shared feeling.

One of the best images of a sympathetic bond between writer and reader comes from *The Elements of Style*, arguably the best book ever written about how to write. Speaking of his old teacher William Strunk, E. B. White wrote that

> Will felt that the reader was in serious trouble most of the time, floundering in a swamp, and that it was the duty of any-one attempting to write English to drain this swamp quickly and get the reader up on dry ground, or at least to throw a rope.[11]

White's metaphor is both vivid and telling. Most important, it shows how the writer tries to enter into the mind of the reader and appreciate whatever difficulties the reader may face. The writer's job (drain the swamp, make things easier) proceeds from the effort—and it is an effort!—to understand what it feels like to be the reader.

Try This
Compose with the reader in mind.

Most of your writing will go through multiple drafts. When and how should you start keeping your reader in mind? I've seen writers become paralyzed by the prospect of facing their audience. I've also seen writers produce work that barely acknowledges that they have readers at all.

Composition is personal: you should do what works best for you. But if you're having trouble at the drafting stage, there are time-honored strategies to try. The most famous may be to imagine that you're writing a letter to your mother or to your best friend in which you explain what you're working on. Or you can design (or imagine designing) a presentation based on your writing task. In each of these cases, you are shifting your attention from yourself to your reader.

But the writer doesn't act just for the reader's sake. The writer has self-serving ends also: if you help the reader, you'll be noticed, remembered, and cited. And if you get cited, you can affect the conversation.

Help your reader, and you help yourself.

Signposting, Quoting, and Other Important Do's and Don'ts

Strunk's rescue rope takes a variety of forms for academic writers. Three important ones are signposting, deduction, and what I'll call story-consciousness. I'll begin with signposting, a discussion that will wrap around to the next chapter, where it will join the other two.

The paragraph I just wrote is an example of signposting. I tried to anticipate your need as reader to want to know what's coming. I gave you an overview to keep you from bailing out on me. I also want you to feel secure in the knowledge of what's coming.

Academic readers value such prospective knowledge. Have you, when you're researching, ever taken a book off the shelf and paged through an article, or the introduction or first chapter of a book, looking for the part where the author summarizes each section of the larger work? You know what this move looks like: "In chapter one I'll cut up the bananas, in chapter two the cherries, in chapter three the berries, and then in chapter four I'll combine them into fruit salad." If you're writing a treatise on cherries, you know that you probably only have to read chapter two.

That summary embedded in the introduction aids immeasurably in the art of getting cited. But that move points to a more important larger point: that authors who employ those summaries are writing the way that the academic reader want to read: for use.*

---

* Some scholarly presses and journals discourage signposting. They should not. Gatekeepers: please examine your own practices and revise them for the benefit of your academic readers. If you do, you'll have more of them.

Moreover, that summary is an example of a wider imperative. Arguments need signposting at different points, especially if they're going to get complicated. When you drive down a hill, you may encounter a sign that looks like this:

The sign warns that the road is going to get curvy, and that the driver had best slow down and pay special attention. Writers need to do no less.

You should signpost if your argument has many complex parts or is otherwise hard to follow. Signpost your argument because you want the reader to understand it, not get lost in it. The mathematician who wrote the following provides a good example of signposting the complexity of an argument:

> In this section, we will make a digression to develop some of the theory of abelian semigroups which will be relevant for K-theory (we will, of course, want to apply the results to the study of $V(A)$ and $Vo(A)$ for a unital ring A).[12]

You don't need to be a mathematician to see how the writer is preparing the reader for what is to come. As simple a signpost as "I will return to this topic later" (which you will see me use in this book, including right now) makes a difference.

Everything you can do to get your reader through your writing will be good for both your reader and you. Signposting can also help you point your reader toward your most important points, lest they be overlooked.

Obstacles

It's a truism that you want to highlight your most important points, but academic writing is loaded with temptations that can lead you away from that goal. For example, beware of bloating and quoting.

Fight bloat in your writing.
Most academic writing is bloated. I mean simply that it takes up more space than it has to, and more space than it should. All of which makes it wearisome: a tiring challenge to read.

Academic writers learn the rewards of bloated prose early on. The instruction starts at least as far back as college, when we all had to fulfill assignments by writing to a set page or word length. We learned all manner of strategies to reach that length: use a block quote when a sentence will work just as well, overexplain, give three pieces of evidence where one will do. Begin once, twice, three times; circle around an ending instead of gliding (or swooping) in for one. Anything to make the necessary length.

We share blame for these practices because each succeeding generation enforces the standards that produce them. The standard 7,500-word essay that features in so many scholarly journals exceeds the desired length of attention of most people, if not their physical attention span itself: it wears a reader out. But unless more academic journals respect shorter pieces—by soliciting them—writers will continue to produce overlong ones.

As writers, we should think in terms of Abraham Lincoln, not the teacher who might have assigned him a twenty-page paper if he were going to college today. Lincoln's Gettysburg address ran to 272 words. Edward Everett, the orator who took the stage before

Lincoln, gave a speech of 13,524. (Point of reference: a double-spaced, typed page contains about 250 words.) Everett said afterward to Lincoln, "I wish that I could flatter myself that I had come as near to the central idea of the occasion, in two hours, as you did in two minutes."

Here's a practical tip: *Instead of wondering what you might gain by including something, ask what you might lose by* not *including it. Often the answer is, not much.*

Draft with prolix abandon if that's your style—you may need to write a lot to start. Then squeeze the excess water weight out of your prose.

Don't block quote if you can avoid it

Those among the initiated may now be wondering whether I've lost my mind. Especially for a college or graduate student, an admonition against block quoting verges on heresy. But if I dissent from the true faith here, it's a church I know well from the inside. I remember many a late night of paper writing when I laid down block quotes to raise my paper upward to the number of pages I needed. Without those bricks, I might be in the library still.

Writers block quote to add length, but they also do it to firm up the ground below them. Block quoting shifts the authority to someone else: "There, they said it," the writer says. "Because I agree, I must be right." I'm not sneering at the need for authority here—students aren't experts, so they need to lean on the shoulders of published writers who are. But there are more concise ways to enlist experts to your side.

Earlier in this chapter I described writing as a journey for two. Block quotations are speed bumps on that journey. Envision your reader's eye dropping down a page. Maybe you're reading closely, or scanning, or moving at some speed in between. Down goes your eye—and it bumps into a block quotation. There the eye stops, as you shift gears and adjust. Then you prepare yourself

Furthermore

"'Quote' is a verb. 'Quotation' is the noun derived from it." I wrote that in the margins of many student papers over many years, whenever I encountered "quote" being used as a noun. But I must be realistic: usage is winning that one. I've given up on correcting that mistake because it's less of a mistake all the time.

Be aware, however, that although our numbers are diminishing, there are still people who care about this distinction.

for a different voice, and move through the block quotation at a different reading pace. That's jarring. For this reason alone, be chary of block quoting.

You should block quote only when one of these two conditions applies:

- *The quotation is so clever or eloquent that you can't say it any better.*
- *You intend to close-read the quotation to explicate it or show how it works* (in other words, you plan to use the quotation as a primary source).

Don't use a block quotation—or any other kind of quotation— just to convey facts. Facts are common property and don't belong to anyone. Convey facts yourself, in your own voice. Save quoting for someone else's opinion, or someone else's clever phrase. The general rule: ***Don't give away the microphone without a good reason.***

The same goes for quoting in general. Avoid it where possible.

Now he's saying that I shouldn't even quote? I hear you mutter. Mostly, yes: ***don't quote unless you have to.***

I'm opposing conventional practice here, but sometimes you have to look at your education as a scaffolding that must be stripped away once the building can stand on its own.

We're taught to quote because it's the most direct way to establish authority: by pointing to a wise, published writer who said it first. But a little of that authority goes a long way. One sage offers "the luggage rule": if you're going to quote other scholars (not as primary sources whose work you mean to analyze, but because they've got insights you want to support yours), make sure they're carrying your luggage and not the other way around.[13]

Another sage suggests that you think of every quoted word as being worth a few cents. How much money do you want to spend on quotations in a piece you're writing? A more prosaic version of the same message: ***Make sure that yours is the voice most heard in your own writing.*** (Unless the source you're working from is profoundly eloquent, in which case, be a big spender.)[14]

In this example, the words of the poet Wordsworth overwhelm the writer's efforts to explain them:

> The speaker remains alone throughout the poem, but by its end this state of being has been transformed into something positive. First he writes, "I wandered lonely as a cloud/That floats on high o'er values and hills,/When all at once I saw a crowd" (lines 1–3). In the last stanza, however, he describes how he feels the "bliss of solitude," suggesting ecstasy and contemplative peace rather than mere loneliness (line 22).

Here is a revised version:

> The speaker remains alone throughout the poem, but by its end this state of being has been transformed into something

positive. While he first describes himself as wandering "lonely as a cloud," in the last stanza he writes of experiencing the "bliss of solitude," which suggests ecstasy and peace rather than mere loneliness (ll. 1, 22).[15]

In the second take, the writer quotes only the parts of the poem that directly support the argument. Not only are Wordsworth's words pared down, so are the writer's own. The result is tighter exposition, with the writer's voice in command.

> **Tip**
> *Don't avoid the verb "to say." Instead, use it a lot.*
>
> How do you render another scholar's ideas? In my years of reading academic writing, I have seen writers describe how their sources "assert," or "posit," or "state," or "assert" things. They also "postulate," "conjecture," "proclaim," "cite," and (very often) "note that."
>
> But they almost never just "say" something. I'm not sure where the resistance to the verb "to say" comes from, though I suspect that academic writers reject it because 1) it sounds too simple; and 2) they worry that repeating it will create monotony.
>
> Ironically, the struggle to avoid admitting that someone "said" something calls attention to the words that substitute for it. If you simply use "say," the reader will glide right through your prose and the repetition will be invisible. If you don't believe me, look at almost any work of fiction that has dialogue.

When you do quote, keep these tips[16] in mind:

Instead of quoting longer excerpts, mix small bits of quotation with paraphrase. This practice keeps you (and not your sources) central, and also provides a consistency of voice and tone that is easier for the reader to follow.

Here, historian J. J. Scarisbrick analyzes the relationships between Henry VIII, archbishop Wolsey, and diplomat Richard Pace by gracefully mixing Scarisbrick's paraphrase and interpretation with quotations from Wolsey:

> Wolsey had a request to make of Pace which throws a precious beam of light on English policy-making and Wolsey's relations with Henry. "By good [policy]" . . . he said, Pace was to persuade the emperor and the Swiss to "make instance to you to be a mean unto the king that they proceed no further but only into the [duchy of] Milan," and that they may be "discharged of the persecuting of the Frenchmen into France." Pace was therefore to squeeze out of the allies a request, addressed to himself, that he should ask Henry to excuse them a major part of their undertaking.[17]

Scarisbrick makes gratifyingly clear who is the storyteller here, and who the characters are in the story.

When you paraphrase, make sure that what you're citing is absolutely clear. Not like this:

> Some scholars argue that Superman is an undocumented Kryptonian, and as such, an illegal immigrant. This proper use of "as such" is rarely seen in academic writing (Schriebmeister).

It isn't clear here whether Schriebmeister was talking about Superman or about the widespread misuse of the phrase "as such" (which is, incidentally, too often used as a placeholder or an empty transition).* Instead:

---

* I'll examine transitions more closely in chapter 2. "As such" invites lazy constructions like this one: "Ancient Greek has an extensive lexicon of violence. As such,

Some scholars argue that Superman is an undocumented Kryp-
tonian, and as such, an illegal immigrant (Schriebmeister). This
proper use of "as such" is rarely seen in academic writing.

The revised version makes clear exactly what the writer is relying
on the source for.

***Play around with the rhythm of interlinear quotation until you
find the sound you like:***

> Patrick Henry thundered, "Give me liberty or give me death!"
> "Give me," thundered Patrick Henry, "liberty or give me death!"
> "Give me liberty or give me," Patrick Henry thundered, "death!"
> "Give me liberty," Patrick Henry thundered, "or give me death!"

When you engage in an exercise like this one, you're listening for
the music in your writing. Try to do this generally, not just when
you're quoting.

Quote to advance your argument. If you say, "When Patrick Henry
says, 'Give me liberty or give me death,' he means a number of
things," you are marking time and deferring thought and assertion.
If you have that habit, become alert to it and revise when you spot
yourself falling into it. ***Don't quote someone saying something
you just said***—that's just another form of repeating yourself. You
can (if you want the outside support) cite that source without
quoting it. Not:

> Thomas Doherty argues that combat films of World War II
> celebrate American pluralism in the form of the melting pot:
> "The melting pot was the insistent theme of the combat film—
> fictional and documentary, ground and air."[18]

Greek tragedians demonstrate that . . ." As such what? The specific connection between
the two parts of the proposition is fuzzy.

Instead, try this:

> Thomas Doherty argues that the World War II combat film—
> "fictional and documentary, ground and air"—celebrates a
> "melting pot" version of American pluralism.

The revised version eliminates redundancy through a combination
of brief quotation and paraphrase.

***Never assume that your reader will find in a quotation the
"obvious" meaning that you see in it.*** Consider the following:

> Julie R. Posselt describes academic disciplines as "both knowl-
> edge markets and knowledge communities. One of the most
> fundamental distinctions between and within disciplines per-
> tains to the forms and foci of knowledge in which scholars
> practice their expertise."[19] These dualities make clear why
> professors are so resistant to workplace change.

Professors may well be resistant to change, but this passage
doesn't deliver the "why" that it claims. The writer assumes that
Posselt's abstractions (markets and communities, form and foci)
explain themselves. They don't. To make things truly clear, the
writer should balance Posselt's abstract point with a concrete illustration of it. A revision might look like this:

> Julie R. Posselt describes academic disciplines as "both knowl-
> edge markets and knowledge communities. One of the most
> fundamental distinctions between and within disciplines per-
> tains to the forms and foci of knowledge in which scholars
> practice their expertise." In other words, when you research
> and teach in a field, you form your professional identity
> within it. Disciplinary expertise defines professors' view of
> themselves as, say, theoretical physicists or experimentalists,
> astronomers or geophysicists. These categories describe not

only research specialties but also researchers' personal sense of what kind of physicist they are. The persistence of these identity-bearing structures makes clear why professors are so resistant to change in the academic workplace.

In the reworked version, the writer describes the extract's meaning by paraphrasing Posselt's own concrete illustration from the field of physics. As a result of this judicious linking of the abstract and the concrete, the reader can finally gain the promised clarity and see how professors' identities may become calcified.

Make sure that the quotation illustrates your point, and practice economy: Quote only the part that supports you directly. This lead-up and extract include unnecessary text:

> Woody Guthrie thrilled to the natural beauty of the United States, but he was revulsed by the callousness and greed he saw alongside it:

> > Guthrie had seen some beautiful things . . . on his travels—waving wheat fields and golden valleys; endless blue skies and redwood forests. He'd seen some awesome things, like enormous, rolling dust clouds and ribbons of highway disappearing to the vanishing point. But he'd also seen some ugly things: high walls and signs proclaiming "Private Property" and "No Trespassing"; lines of hungry and destitute people, seeking relief; vigilantes and deputies forcing them to go where they didn't want to go. All of these went into the song that, he concluded, was about a land that had been "made for you and me"—for whomever "you and me" happened to be.[20]

This block quotation contains far more verbiage than the writer needs to make the point, and the unnecessary details obscure the necessary ones. Instead, try trimming and paraphrasing:

Woody Guthrie thrilled to the natural beauty of the United States, but he was revulsed by the callousness and greed he saw alongside it: "high walls and signs proclaiming 'Private Property' and 'No Trespassing'; lines of hungry and destitute people, seeking relief; vigilantes and deputies forcing them to go where they didn't want to go." Guthrie put the ugly alongside the beautiful in his most famous song "about a land that had been 'made for you and me'—for whomever 'you and me' happened to be."

The revised version focuses more sharply because the reduced quotation makes the writer's point right away. It also gets rid of the block quotation, an improvement in itself.

The only correct use for single quotes is to indicate a quotation within a quotation. It's not accepted American English usage (meaning that if you're writing for a U.S. audience, it's just wrong) to indicate the difference between quoted words and slang (or your own invented expressions) by using double quotes for one and single quotes for the other. Thus:

According to Thomas Tangerine, "the best and only faithful form of citrus love is what Charlotte Cherimoya calls the 'grapefruit grasp.'" Only thus may we witness fruitful fidelity.[21]

Tip

Economize: Don't repeat the titles of your sources.

Avoiding block quotations isn't the only way to save time and space. You also don't need to list the title of your secondary source when it already appears in your list of works cited. Not:

As Tristam Tinpeach explains in her "Platter Composition: The Delicate Art and Sweet Science of Fruit Salad," the need

> "to layer bananas on top is absolutely essential, as the watermelon will otherwise drip all over them."

The name of the article gums up the flow of the sentence here. Try instead:

> Tristam Tinpeach says that it's "absolutely essential" to place your bananas on top, in order to keep the watermelon from dripping on them.

In this second example, the removal of the clunky title, together with the substitution of paraphrase for some of the quotation, allows the sentence to flow.

In the same self-centered spirit (because you're the writer at the center of your work), *limit the presence of your sources in your own text*. You need to acknowledge where you enter the conversation, of course: the person you may be agreeing and disagreeing with, whose work you may be building on or revising. But you don't need to summarize that work at length. Describe it only as much as is necessary for your own purposes. Not:

> According to Alexandra Apricot, [and now ten lines describing Apricot's aggressive approach to pitting stone fruit].

Instead:

> Alexandra Apricot recommends removing the pits from stone fruit with explosive charges. [and here you can add a few details.]

You have your own story to tell: Be mindful of distracting from it. In the next chapter I'll examine that story more closely, and show how to use it.

CHAPTER 2

Everything Is a Story

The Argument Is a Story

Human beings are storytelling animals. We use stories to understand the world and ourselves, and we tell stories to communicate that understanding.

Even when we don't realize we're doing it, we're telling stories. The instruction booklet explaining how to jump your car's dead battery is a story. The recipe you follow to make dinner is a story. And so is the academic essay you read or write—or at least it should be.

In academic writing, the argument makes an essay an essay. Argument is the currency of the realm, the measure of what a piece of writing is worth. Most of all, argument is what academic readers read for. Knowing how to make a good argument (or thesis) is an academic writer's central skill, which is why it's taught as the main goal of first-year English ("Composition"), the gateway course to college education.

Too many academic arguments get in their own way. Some arrive cloaked in scaffolding that needed to be stripped away before delivery. Others lack the structural integrity to stand atop their own evidence—or they topple due to lack of that evidence. Others groan under the weight of unnecessary digressions that drag them down and make them hard to follow. Arguments easily turn convoluted, involuted, and lead-footed. This chapter will show you how to make arguments with clean lines, clear structure, and strong foundations.

Here's the first rule for how to do that: remember that *all arguments are also stories*. The way to make an argument sticky is to keep in mind that you're telling a story. That's my argument—and my story—and I'm sticking to it. This chapter is a story about how to tell a better story.*

Remember that a story need not have a whimsical plot. In academic writing, it usually should not. Jerry Seinfeld's streaming series *Comedians in Cars Getting Coffee* is an example of a simple linear story. Every episode unfolds in the same way: Jerry and his guest get into a car, they buy coffee, and they drive back. That's a story, because even a structure that basic creates narrative expectation. That expectation can then be exploited; in this case, it becomes a skeleton that the interesting stuff—the banter between the comedians—is attached to. *Comedians in Cars* is literally story-driven.

What kind of story should an academic writer tell?

The answer: a straightforward one. To illustrate, let's start with the counterexample of Billy Wilder's classic film noir *Sunset Boulevard*. The movie begins with a murder victim floating in a Hollywood swimming pool. "Maybe you'll like to hear the facts, the whole truth," says the narrator in a voice-over. "If so, you've come to the right party."

Wilder makes a couple of noteworthy moves here. First, he signals that he's going to tell a story that explains the dead body in the pool. Second, he doesn't tell you everything about it. Most important, he's not telling you who the dead man is. (If you want to know, here's a spoiler.[1]) The deliberate omission serves the story's purpose: like most crime stories, *Sunset Boulevard* has a surprise ending.

---

* The reason that encyclopedia entries make such dull reading is that they generally don't tell a story. They just pass along information as efficiently as possible.

The deceptive approach of crime stories—which often trick the audience—doesn't make much sense for scholars who write to teach their work to readers. Spoiler alert, then: academic writers should *not* try to write their own *Sunset Boulevard*. But you can still customize Wilder's two opening moves:

First, write from your main idea, not to it. If there's a body floating in the pool, start with it. Don't describe the pool first. In other words, start with whatever your writing is most deeply about. If you're ultimately trying to explain the function of the narrator in *Uncle Tom's Cabin*, start with the narrator and save your relevant but secondary historical riffs on abolitionism, proslavery, and domestic feminism for the body of your piece.

The second half of this rule is: ***Let text invoke context, not the other way around***. If you're explaining literature, start with literature. But if you're doing history (say, offering a fresh historical analysis of antislavery thought inspired by *Uncle Tom's Cabin*), start with history, though you can use a line or two from the novel as an opening frame if it takes you to the history right away. Putting your main idea up front and then stepping back to take in the context frames that main idea. This move makes it immediately and structurally clear to the reader what's most important to you, and what overarching objective will organize that follows.

Furthermore

Think of the primacy of text over context as though you were a painter making a portrait. You should sketch in the sitter before you turn to the background, because the sitter is the reason for the picture, the focus of the viewer's eye.

Second, you can reveal the main idea in parts. But prioritize deduction. The technical terms here are induction (writing toward your main idea) and deduction (writing from it). Deductive writing puts the thesis first. Inductive writing builds to a reveal of the main idea. The approaches can be combined (stay tuned for how), but now we arrive at this rule:

Write deductively for academic readers. (I'll qualify this rule with a "most of the time.") Remember the main point of chapter 1: that academic readers read for use value. They want to know what you're arguing, and how. Be generous to them and offer some help. Tell them quickly what they can expect.*

So get your thesis out there early. Explain how your argument will unfold. (That explanation is your "methodology.") Give the use-driven reader a sense of what is to come so that she can decide how to approach your work.

Tip

Define your key terms early.

Your opening is also the place to define key terms, including any jargon you may be relying on (or that you invented for the occasion). I'll have a lot more to say about jargon in the next chapter. Here, I followed my own advice when I defined "inductive" and "deductive" for my own purposes at the outset.

Make deduction your guiding approach. You don't want to ambush a use-driven reader with a surprise that will make them want to go back and review everything they just read. That's fun after you watch *Sunset Boulevard* or read Agatha Christie's *Murder on the Orient Express*, but academic readers don't want to cover everything all over again. You want to create an efficient reading experience for them.

---

* An acronym popular in government communication, which often needs to get to the point right away, is BLUF: "Bottom Line Up Front."

Here's an extended example:

Let's say that you're planning a three-part argument about the Topkapi people of the South Seas.

First, they build their culture on theft.

Second, the origins of Topkapi thievery stem from their attraction to precious stones, whose timeless appeal becomes clear through study of Topkapi myth and legend.

Finally, you'll show that the latter-day disintegration of Topkapi culture results from the tendency of anthropologists who study the Topkapi to steal their jewels from them. You'll base the first two parts of your argument on existing scholarship (which you'll synthesize), but the last point about the klepto-anthropologists is something that you figured out by reading the diaries of anthropologists in an online archive.*

The basic architecture of this (or any) argument depends on coherent structure and sequence. You can present the first part of this argument—or perhaps the first two parts together—to start. After you've explained and supported the first two propositions, you'll be ready to introduce and support the third one. If you started with the third part of the argument, you would be telling the story out of order, and it probably wouldn't make coherent sense to anyone but you.

Try This
Reverse-outlining

If you're wondering whether you've structured your argument soundly, reverse-outline it. That is, outline it after the fact and see whether the outline makes sense to you.

---

* In case you're wondering, I'm making all of this up. Topkapi is the name of a palace in Istanbul and the eponym for an excellent jewel heist movie from 1964.

A persuasive argument depends on many writerly virtues:

You need to make clear connections between the parts of your argument—which requires not only a sound forensic structure in the first place, but also good transitions.

There needs to be logic (especially a narrative logic) to your approach.

You need to make the boundaries of your own contribution—your idea, as compared to what others have already argued—clear and distinct. Gerald Graff and Cathy Birkenstein have named this move "they say/I say."[2]

"They say/I say" points to a writer's need to show what's at stake. In this imaginary case, you must show why someone else should care about what you've discovered about Topkapi culture. Why does your argument matter? Or, more simply: so what? You therefore need to place your claims into the larger context of what's already known of the Topkapi and certain related subjects that may be relevant to your argument. Some possibilities: the psychology of theft, the allure of jewels, the impulse to collect things, or the dissolution of cultural bonds, to name a few.

Through this presentation, *you should keep your reader oriented, so she always knows her place in your argument.* (I described this with the extended metaphor of the chariot ride in chapter 1, and I'll elaborate further presently.) It's not worth saying something if nobody can understand you. And if you can only be understood with difficulty, you will soon exhaust your reader. So explain to your audience what you're doing, either before you start or while you're doing it.

To accomplish all of these things is to tell a story. *Your story needs two components above all: sound structure and concern for the reader.* Each of these affects the other. Both of them apply to good writing, from an entire book down to each sentence that it contains.

There are techniques and rules for presenting an argument well. I'll cover some important ones here. The overall structure of my presentation—the story I'm telling—will move from the larger elements to the smaller ones. I'll consider some of the judgment calls that academic writers make in the beginnings, middles, and ends of their arguments. Throughout, I'll continue my discussion of signposting (which I started at the end of the last chapter, and a technique I'm engaging in right now)—because I want to be deductive here myself. Let's begin with the whole before turning to its parts:

Don't Write It from Beginning to End

The artist Stephen Wiltshire specializes in panoramic cityscapes. After he receives a commission, Wiltshire will view a city during a brief helicopter flight. Then, working entirely from memory, he will fill a room with a meticulously detailed drawing. Because his creation is often filmed in process, it also becomes a kind of performance art. One of the most compelling aspects of the performance is that the artist works from one side of the room to the other, drawing without sketching first, almost like a living computer printer. Wiltshire can do this because his brain works atypically. (He was diagnosed with autism at age three.)[3]

Now imagine writing the way Wiltshire draws. You'd have to start at the beginning and work your way sequentially to the end. In order to do that, you would have to see everything in your head to start with. Most people don't think that way. And when it comes to larger writing projects, most people can't.

Yet so many academic writers try to write from beginning to end. Some of them never stop doing it. One student writer recently confessed to me that he feels guilty if he doesn't have "the perfect paper in my head" when he sits down to write. "My writing comes out messy," he said, "and I feel like I'm doing something wrong." I used to write like that when I was in college, composing in longhand. Because I would constantly double back to add and subtract things, my manuscripts would end up so cluttered and complicated that I was the only one who could decipher them.

My repeated returns to insert and delete show that I actually could *not* compose from beginning to end. In fact, I was revising as I went along because things kept occurring to me. My writing process unfolded that way because for me—and for most writers—*writing is thinking, not just a record of your thoughts*. Only by actually writing do you figure out what you want to say, and how you should say it.

Try This

Because writing is a disciplined form of thinking, I suggest you plan your writing task by actually writing, not by reflecting on it before you sit down. What surfaces through your pen or keyboard may pleasantly surprise you.

I write because I don't know what I think until I read what I say.   **—ATTRIBUTED TO FLANNERY O'CONNOR**

It follows that you should avoid starting right at the beginning. You can best introduce your work when you can see it whole—but you can't see it whole until you've worked through the middle and brought the end into sight. Here's a compositional tip: after you outline or otherwise get a sense of your overall task, **start writing at the point where you're most confident of what you want to say**. Keep writing until you're less sure, or you reach a natural resting point. Then look for another point where you feel secure about your ideas, and write from there. Keep creating chunks of exposition in this way. After you have a few, you'll probably start to see how they fit together.

My own writing got easier, faster, and better when I started writing this way. Writing from the middle also helped me take on longer projects—including this book, which I did not write in order.

Furthermore

Working on a long essay years before the internet, a young John McPhee encountered difficulty moving from the notes he had taken to the actual writing of the piece. Then he balanced a thirty-two-foot-long plank across two sawhorses. He arranged his notecards on top of it and moved them around until he found a good order for them. Decades later, he recalled, "Nothing in that arrangement changed across the many months of writing."

McPhee's experience shows that it helps to see the whole of your work at once. Unfortunately, computers only display a screen's worth at a time. Tip: find your own equivalent of what McPhee did. Print out your piece, outline it on a whiteboard, or find your own technology to allow you to see your work in its entirety. Doing this will aid your composition and revision together.

From the whole, let's now move to the parts of a piece of writing.

Let's Start with the Title . . .

. . . because that's where your reader will start.

Always title your work. Always. Even if you're writing a draft, give it a title. First, the title introduces your work to your audience. It's your chance to shape a first impression. That's an opportunity you should always jump at, in both writing and life.

Second, titling your work requires *you* to look back at it and consider it as a whole. It's a form of reverse outlining—a way of asking yourself, "What did I just do?" Finding a title that fits your work is one way to test whether you've accomplished what you set out to do. So title your work in progress: doing so will show your work to yourself.

Think of your title as an invitation to your reader to a gathering at your house. Your title should allow the reader to answer the question, "Do I want to come to this party?"

To get the guests through the door, your invitation should be welcoming and generous. To get the greatest number of guests, your invitation should also be clear. Is this a cocktail hour? A dinner party? How much can you say about what you're planning to serve? You can't expect to please everyone, but you'll want to make sure that your offerings appeal to the people who most need them.

For Example

To create a simple, direct title, you may have to eliminate an opening phrase that sits before a colon. Such a title usually looks like this:

> Fancy phrase (sometimes a quotation): Prosaic explanation of what the article or book is really about.

For example:

> *Golden Gulag: Prisons, Surplus, Crisis, and Opposition in Globalizing California.*

Another example uses a neologism to describe how bacteria will copy the DNA of a virus, which enables them to fight off the virus:

> "Microbiomimesis: Bacteria, Our Cognitive Collaborators."

Put a colon in your title if you wish—many writers obviously do. (I've done it myself.) But understand that the practice is becoming timeworn, so if you're going to make a potentially clichéd move, rescue yourself from cliché by doing it in an interesting and original way. At the very least, the term on the left side of the colon should be clever, as in the examples above.

For the same reasons, be likewise wary of titling your work with a gerund ("Exploring [your topic's name here]"), a technique that one very good writer calls "Ruining My Day."

Simplest is often best. I work with an editor at a scholarly press who regularly changes the titles of accepted book manuscripts when they enter production. His replacements are invariably prosaic: they aim to communicate what the book is about in plain terms, without fancy quotations in front of a colon. These practices are followed in other fields too. Here are the titles of four of the most often-cited articles on climate change. They're gratifyingly clear:

"Predictive Habitat Distribution Models in Ecology";
"Extinction Risk from Climate Change";
"Evidence for General Instability of Past Climate from a 250-Kyr Ice-Cor Record";
"Global Analyses of Sea Surface Temperature, Sea Ice, and Night Marine Air Temperature since the Late 19th Century."[4]

Along the same clean and simple lines, I like this one very much: "The World's Largest Omnivore Is a Fish."[5] Titling your writing after what it's about will bore your audience only if your subject is boring to start with.

Now to what lies below the title, the argument itself:

The Architecture of Arguments

Your title will communicate your subject, but not necessarily your argument. Scholarly arguments are often complex, and they frequently have multiple parts. But certain qualities are common to all of them.

All scholarly arguments—in every field—identify a topic, problem, or question and then explore it.[6] The goal is to answer questions raised by the topic, problem, or question. If you're successful, your reader will see the subject in a new way. Not all arguments will "solve" the problem. Actually, few of them will. You can't expect to "solve" reptilian courtship behavior or deliver the last word on Plato's *Republic*. But as an academic writer, you can make progress and add to the common store.

> **Tip**
>
> Graduate students and other nervous writers may worry about whether they belong in a published conversation, so they will often diminish their claims. For example, they may claim that their writing "fills a gap" instead of saying something important in its own right.
>
> ***Believe in your argument as something that matters.*** Instead of trying to squeeze into a small space, think in terms of the stakes of your claim, and why it's important. If you don't stand up for your argument, then why should your reader care about it?

In your opening, present the question or problem. Then turn it into an argument. There are countless ways to do this, but here's one common one.[7]

Begin with an example. To return to my hypothetical, you could describe a particularly flagrant Topkapi jewel theft.

Then invoke the what the example teaches us. You could explain how theft plays a role in all of Topkapi culture's important rituals, from baby naming to funerals. You can further explain how jewel mining in the river basin in Topkapi territory correlates with increased theft within Topkapi culture—and with the creation of Topkapi myths about jewels.

From the implications, you invoke the problem, or question, that drives your research. What does Topkapi jewel theft signify within Topkapi culture? What does it tell us about the tribe, its history, its current situation? You might discuss why these implications have been important to anthropologists who study the Topkapi, and what earlier scholars have thought about the Topkapi. You'll provide a more thorough discussion of those earlier scholars in your literature review, about which more shortly.

> **Tip**
> *Don't make your introduction too detailed.*
>
> Your introduction should present your argument, not make it. If you write an introduction that's so detailed that it feels like a complete argument in itself, you may feel a reluctance to repeat yourself further in the main body of what follows. Remember that the goal of **the introduction is to identify a path and provide an on-ramp so that the reader can start traveling that path with you.**

From the problem, you reach your argument: that jewel theft not only provides mythological foundation for Topkapi culture, but also allows its members to differentiate themselves from neighboring tribes. *Here you can preview your final claim*: that as jewel theft has declined among the Topkapi, the tribe has abandoned its endogamous practices and even its sacred lands—and anthropologists may trace this shift to Topkapi contact with their own greedy anthropological predecessors, who learned many of these things in the first place, and who adopted the practice of jewel theft themselves.

You can see how these steps form a story. It's a story of what you've learned about the Topkapi, and how you learned it—and why it's worth paying attention to. The end of your story is you're your contribution to the subject, and why it matters.

Only by identifying an important problem or question can you justify asking a reader to continue reading. Only if you organize the problem into a story (that is, find its narrative logic) will the reader want to continue reading.

Furthermore

"You have to make the reader feel that *it matters* what he's doing."   **—NOTE TO SELF BY ROBERT CARO**

That's pretty good advice for any writer to follow.

Address Counterargument

All arguments have counterarguments. If they didn't, they would be statements of fact, not arguments at all. You need to acknowledge counterargument in order to be fully persuasive. When you counterargue, you anticipate objections and show that you've thought of them, thereby illustrating that your position is based on a thorough consideration of all of the relevant facts, not just the selected ones that support you. That's why in the world of litigation, lawyers will often cite the other side's best evidence in their opening statements, to show that they're going to rebut all of the assertions against them, not just some of them.

The author of this passage acknowledges counterargument and fairly critiques it at the same time:

Latin America, which . . . undertook a considerable amount of "structural reform," ended up growing slower not only relative to Asian countries but also relative to its own historical benchmarks. . . . To downplay the importance of these disappointments requires that we go through a number of contortions, none of which is particularly convincing. One counterargument is that countries in Latin America and Africa . . . have simply not undertaken enough reform. What is "enough" is obviously in the eyes of the beholder, but this claim seems to me to be grossly unfair to the scores of leaders in Latin America and

Africa who have spent considerable political capital in pursuit of Washington Consensus–style reforms. The weakness of the claim is also evident from the ease with which temporary successes in these countries have been ascribed to the reforms being implemented.[8]

The critique in this second example, which focuses on "Why Japan is haunted by its past and Germany is not," unnecessarily belittles the author's predecessors:

> Some scholars, such as Lieberson (1991), claim that qualitative analysis is a hopelessly blunt tool for solving a puzzle like the one posed in this book. But I disagree. Designed and executed properly, a comparative case study can be just as useful as a quantitative (or large-N statistical) analysis. The trick is to follow Mill's method of difference: investigate cases that differ significantly in their outcomes, and then isolate the causal factor or explanatory variable by controlling for others. That is exactly what I have done here.[9]

When we look closely, we can see that the phrase "some scholars" insinuates a lack of qualification (that such people aren't numerous, aren't authoritative, and aren't as specialized as historians or economists). The hyperbole of "hopelessly" overstates the counterargument in order to refute it more easily. And the shift in register—between the folksy common sense of "the trick is" and the exclusionary jargon of "large-N statistical analysis" and "Mill's method of difference"—casts the speaker as possessing a total fluency in the discipline that his antagonists lack.

You need not diminish your opponents in order to argue with them. In fact, your own work will gain in magnitude if you acknowledge the value of the work you successfully oppose.

How to Structure a Comparison

Many an argument takes the form of putting two distinct elements in comparison. It's easy for comparisons to get clunky if you spend too much time on one element before moving to the other. Moreover, if you spend too much time describing the first item in your comparison before moving to the second, you effectively delay your argument—because your claim lies in the comparison itself.

It therefore behooves you to *start comparing as soon as you can*. Not: "The 1989 Exxon Valdez oil spill wrecked the marine environment," followed by pages on the Valdez disaster, and then, "By contrast, the Love Canal ecological disaster discovered in 1978 . . ." Instead, introduce both aspects of your subject as soon as you can: "The Exxon Valdez oil spill, unlike the Love Canal disaster, reveals . . ." *Move back and forth between your ideas, subordinating first one and then the other—and always keeping both in view.*[10]

There's a general principle lurking here. The same back-and-forth method also works if you're analyzing a position and its counterargument. This isn't exactly a comparison, but the technique of toggling back and forth between claim and counterclaim works well here, too—and in most cases when you're looking closely at more than one thing at once.

The Geometry of Argument

If an argument has a clear structure, you should be able to visualize that structure.

The triangle below diagrams an inductive argument: that is, one that proceeds toward its main idea. This method works well for a mystery story, where the argument is something like "The butler did it." It fits an academic inquiry less well. Inductive structures ask the reader to keep an increasing number of ideas in mind before the writer finally ties them together. A use-driven academic reader can't easily keep all of these ideas in suspension, especially if they're dense or complicated—which, in scholarly arguments, they often are.[11]

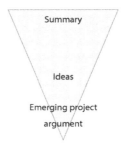

For Example

The authors of "The Political and Emotional Economy of Violence in US Inner City Narcotics Markets" employ this risky inductive structure. The article begins with a dramatic field note from the inner city, then gives a novelistic account of the streets of Philadelphia. The authors then review theoretical perspectives on violence before finally advancing the thesis that "extreme eruptions of violence are imposed onto the logics of everyday sociability among ambitious, unemployed youth in the US inner city" by dysfunctional public policy and government mismanagement. You can see how this structure demands a lot of focused attention from a reader looking for an argument.

You can expect more patience from a book reader—and many book authors bank on that. Sarah Schulman's introduction to *Gentrification of the Mind: Witness to a Lost Imagination* begins with the author's personal anecdote about nearly crashing her car while overhearing a radio broadcast about the history of AIDS. This recollection prompts her to summarize facts and figures of the AIDS epidemic and her personal experience as an AIDS activist before she finally presents her thesis: that the history of AIDS has been obscured because it has been overshadowed by consumerism and gentrification.

On the other hand, this triangle represents a deductive argument:

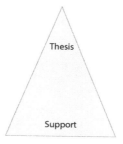

A deductive presentation works *from* the thesis, which gives the reader an organizing principle from early on.* Deduction thus anchors your presentation. The reader will understand your supporting ideas (including your evidence) in relation to your argument.

For Example

The book *Domination and the Arts of Resistance* begins with a thesis: that "the dissembling of the weak in the face of power" has a "strategic dimension" as a political force. The author, James C. Scott, then elaborates this argument with literary examples, before unpacking the political nature of petty acts such as sabotage, foot-dragging, evasion, false compliance, pilfering, feigned ignorance, and slander.

All academic writing should be thesis-driven, but deductive presentations accommodate that goal most explicitly. A deductive approach also allows you to modify your argument as it unfolds, perhaps by adding parts to it, as in the Topkapi example. When you

---

* A forceful op-ed essay frequently follows this structure. Because op-eds rarely exceed eight hundred words, their writers usually limit themselves to one main point. Longer academic essays rely on more complex deductively-based structures that can accommodate clusters of related ideas.

spotlight your argument within your larger structure in this way, you ask your reader to keep an eye on the most important thing.

Because writing is thinking (and not just a record of thoughts you already have), you will often write your way from one idea to another. That's a happy event when it happens: you witness your thoughts becoming deeper and more complex. When a second part of your argument (or maybe a second argument) emerges from the first one, it may initially look like this:

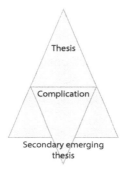

In the diagram, we can see that the writer's discussion of the primary argument has produced a second, likely related, idea. That second idea is emerging from the first, but it's emerging upside-down. That is, complications of the first (deductive) argument are coalescing into a separate thought that is moving toward its own thesis, at the bottom point of the second triangle.

Tip

This example of writing your way toward a second idea from your first shows particularly clearly why *you should write your introduction last*.

To write it first, you need to be able to envision the whole of your work. But writing is thinking—so you won't know what the whole looks like until you're finished, and the intro you worked so hard on probably won't apply anymore.

Try This

Keep an open file labeled "intro" into which you toss all of your loose ends—the misplaced overview, the odd phrase or paragraph that doesn't fit—as you compose. Return to that file at the end and you'll often find a lode of raw material for your introduction.

The second thought arises inductively: the support generates the idea rather than the other way around. That's a potentially confusing structure, especially because the support of the first idea (the main argument) blurs into the complications that are producing the second idea. If you write a draft whose structure combines deduction and induction in this way, you'll likely need to revise with the reader's needs in mind. The reader benefits from a deductive structure, which might look like this:

Tip

Revision creates good structure.

Don't expect sound forensic structures to emerge fully formed. It often takes several drafts for them to come into view. It's your shaping, shearing, pasting, and polishing that will make them visible to you.

This diagram pictures the complex thesis structure of most good academic writing. It shows a writer in command of the subject who has written (and revised!) so that one main idea organically gives way to a second, related idea. The argument unfolds in related parts, revealing its complexity, and *each part starts deductively, with its own main idea.*

> **For Example**
>
> In her review "Getting In and Out," Zadie Smith crafts a complicated two-part argument about the contradictory nature of American race relations. She does this by structuring her essay in two parts: by analyzing first Jordan Peele's film *Get Out* and then Dana Schutz's painting *Open Casket.*

You can see how there's an inductive aspect to this development: the idea shaping the top triangle brings forth the idea that creates the second triangle. But the presentation of each idea is deductive. Note, too, that this structure can repeat itself: the second idea may give way to a third, and so on. That's one way that papers become theses or dissertations, and articles become books.

This geometry shows the necessity of logical structure. The more complicated your idea, the more necessary it is to use a structure that will allow you to present it clearly, in a way that your reader will be able to follow and understand. Building a sound, well-sequenced argument that flows logically is one of the fundamental ways that you take care of your reader.

Taking Care of the Reader in Mid-Argument

Writers invite the reader to board their train of thought. (I described a chariot ride in chapter 1, but transportation technology has advanced now that we've reached chapter 2.) Wearing both the engineer's and conductor's hats, you aim to keep the reader moving forward and comfortable until the end of your journey together. To do that, you'll need to anticipate her questions and concerns and give her a logical basis for making sense of your claims.

For Example

In *Sport in Capitalist Society*, Tony Collins asks his thesis questions up front:

> Why did modern sport emerge in Britain? What forces propelled it around the world? Why has it become a vehicle for nationalism? What made sport such a bastion of masculinity? How did the spirit of amateurism rise and eventually fall? Why have major sporting events in the twenty-first century become synonymous with authoritarian control and corporate excess?

Then he summarizes his argument and its structure at the same time:

> *Sport in Capitalist Society* seeks to answer these and other questions by examining the history of sport over the last 300 years. It argues that modern sport is as much a product of capitalism as the factory, the stock exchange, or the unemployment line. Modern sport emerged in eighteenth-century Britain as part of the growth of a commercial entertainment industry, and sport's binary world of winners and losers matched perfectly the cultural dynamic of capitalism.

After this opening move, the author goes on to summarize the individual arguments of each chapter.

Foreground and Background

Put yourself in the reader's place and ask: *What does the reader need to know to understand the argument? When does the reader need to know it?*

Sometimes you'll need to provide some background (or context) in order to make a key point. That background may be brief, and in that event you can integrate it into your analysis:

> Diamonds were rare in the Topkapi mines, and so were greatly prized. The great diamond theft of 1964 therefore gained special notoriety.

The first statement provides background for the second.

Another subject may demand a more involved context. If you're writing about predatory lending by today's for-profit colleges in the United States, you may need to outline the history of federal student loans in order to make your point. Because that history may fill a few pages, you might choose to place that background into a separate section—while also making clear why you're asking the reader to follow you as you travel along this tangent from your main point.

How can you tell the difference between a brief contextual point that you can present along the way and a longer one that merits its own section? That's a judgment call: you'll often have to write your way to the best answer, and that answer will often depend on how specialized your audience is (so what needs brief explanation, and what merits a more lengthy discussion?). Many is the writer who during revision 1) has needed to expand a brief remark into a fully-researched subsection; and 2) has written such a section and then discovered later that it should be compressed to a couple of sentences, sent to the endnotes, or banished altogether. The more you practice, the better your judgment will get—as long as you keep looking at your work from the reader's point of view.

Furthermore

"There is no good writing, only good rewriting."

One sign of the value of this axiom is that it has been attributed to so many different people. If you find out who originally said it, please let me know.

Here are some related ways to help the reader:

Signposts and Transitions

An academic writer's most important task is to make a specific, coherent argument. In order to do that, you should **spotlight your main claims.** Burying or obscuring central insights makes them harder for the reader to track. You may have trouble tracking them as well, which can leave them underdeveloped. If the reader and the writer both struggle, the argument will surely be confusing to follow and hard to read.

Tip

To help you understand the reader's point of view, **read your work aloud,** either alone or to a peer. *Read it slowly and expressively,* with a pen at hand to take notes.

Listen to the *sound* of your writing. If you have trouble reading a sentence out loud, your reader will likely have trouble with it on the page.

Listen for the *sense* of your writing. Do you hear the argument unfurling? If you can sense yourself getting lost, there's a good chance that your reader will get lost, too.

Look at the problem from the reader's point of view. As I've said, academic arguments are often complicated, so readers need all the help they can get. Signposts, transitions, and syntheses provide that help because they communicate structure. (Transition words such as *furthermore*, *moreover*, or *however* can provide fallback help, but if you write a logically constructed argument, you won't need them very often.) I keep talking about signposts because they work so well to inform and direct the reader. They're like the color blazes on the trees of a hiking trail. For example:

A **Guiding signpost** communicates what you've done, and what you're about to do:

> "With the history of Topkapi theft culture in mind, I now turn to the different kinds of stones they steal."

> "The water shortages in Los Angeles point to overpopulation, and with it how existing water law invited that overpopulation."

Connecting signposts show how one set of ideas relates to another set:

> "Viewing chewing-gum collectors through the lens of disgust theory shows why the sports memorabilia market has become a decadent spectacle."

> "Although the president and prime minister of Freedonia differ on the legitimacy of horse racing, they agree on the necessity of breeder's guides."

Emphasis signposts the most important aspects of your argument:

> "Implicit in Baseball Commissioner Kennesaw Mountain Landis's racism is the key question of why the team owners who employed him let him engage in it."

"The important variable to notice when tracing the rise of crappie sport fishing is the corresponding decline of the commercial harvest of crappies."

Step-back signposts show the connection of the part to the whole: how an idea or piece of evidence connects to your larger argument:

"Doe-Eye O'Dellsky's bunco steering exemplifies the perverse logic of frontier materialism during the nineteenth century."

"When strolling couples start poisoning pigeons in the park, we witness the disastrous effects of the postwar liberal consensus."

Good signposts communicate the status of your argument at a given stage. Signposts often combine with transitions, but the two aren't the same. Signposts address the state of the argument (or section of the argument), so they may communicate how far it has reached and what it has achieved. As you can see, many of the sample signposts above also synthesize what has come before as the argument gets ready to take a turn.

The reader benefits from all of these moves. Signposts can affirm the reader's own experience of your argument, or they may resettle a reader whose attention has temporarily veered off. Effective signposts can answer these questions:

- Why is this idea important to the larger argument? How does this idea connect to the thesis?
- Where is this claim leading? How does this claim motivate points to be made later?
- How is this claim related to previous or subsequent ones? What's the relationship between this claim and the previous claim? The following one?
- How much of the argument has been made so far, and what part of it has yet to be made? At what stage are we in the

argument? Here, you might add examples beginning with "first," "second," etc., and "in conclusion."

Here are some other signposts:

To further build on an idea:

The names of Starbucks drinks took on special significance among youthful consumers, as if they were . . .

Similar to military academies, cooking schools have an immersiveness that . . .

To develop one idea into another:

Because of the abundance of alligators, pet store revenues increased . . .

As a result of pandemic-related shortages, the black market in toilet paper thrived . . .

In the same way that snakes shed their skins, countries . . .

The collapse of the embargo points to the important principle of . . .

To develop a contrast:

Unlike a clown's nose, a mosquito's proboscis evolved according to . . .

In seeming opposition to Lina Wertmüller's flamboyant battles of the sexes, Whit Stillman's mannered sparring . . .

To complicate an idea:

Despite its inexpensiveness and ease of use, the sphygmomanometer has yet to . . .

Even though most Californians had never seen a gibbon, the animal gained a mythological reputation there when . . .

Should You Divide Your Work into Sections?

Sometimes. Sections (with headings) can help your reader see how your argument is unfolding. Section markers also provide places for readers to rest and glance back at the ground they just covered.

If you segment your argument, its sections should support your larger claims. But don't create too many sections. If you divide your work into Section McNuggets, you will tire out most readers. They can take only so many stops and starts.

Books or theses, even short ones, almost always need sections. Essays focused on ideas that are very closely and organically related may not need explicit sections at all. In this case, clear transitions between ideas may suffice to keep the structure clear and the reader oriented within it.

Talk About What You're Not Talking About

All topics—including all problems and all arguments—need boundaries. As the writer, you'll set them for your own reasons. These reasons can include practicality: you don't want to turn a single essay (or dissertation, or book) into a life's work. Consequently, you will sometimes choose to stop short of potentially relevant ideas or examples that connect to your topic. In the case of the imaginary Topkapi example, you may choose not to talk about the (also imaginary) South American Rififi tribe, even though that tribe also engages in ritual thievery. Maybe you're omitting the Rififi because they only steal from other tribes and not each other, or maybe just because you don't have time for them.

All academic writers (but especially those who have something on the line, like graduate students and young professors) need to show what they are *not* talking about—and to provide a rationale for those choices. Do this to mark out what lies outside the scope of your argument. Or do it to head off the charge that you may have forgotten something, which, if true, would hurt your credibility.

For Example

There is no space in this article to take up the consequences of these theories for the study of the history of the religion of Israel except to note that they cast doubt on the possibility of our knowing anything about it.   **—R. N. WHYBRAY**

So *flag what you* don't *write about, lest someone think you don't know it.* Supply a brief explanation for your decision. In this way, you're doing what the author of a Last Will and Testament does when he leaves a single dollar to a shunned relative. That dollar shows that he hasn't forgotten that person, and precludes the possibility of a challenge to his will on that basis.

The need to show what you know brings us to another vital convention of academic writing:

The Literature Review

It's your job as an academic writer to summarize the previous work on your topic to show what you're adding to the conversation. Different disciplines have different conventions for doing this.

For Example

Scientific literature also includes articles where the literature review is the star of the show. Camille Parmesan and Gary Yohe's "A Globally Coherent Fingerprint of Climate Change Impacts across Natural Systems," one of the most cited sources in climate-change studies, is an analytical literature review. The authors analyze other studies on birds, butterflies, and alpine herbs and argue on the basis of that analysis that climate change is broadly affecting the survival of species.

Scientific articles typically open with an abstract (so that the reader can see the argument and methodology encapsulated) and then plunge right into what is called the "literature review," in which the writers identify previous work that's relevant to their own and summarize its findings. Readers of scientific articles expect that "Here's what everyone else did" will open the story and lead to "Here's what we did."

The authors of "Discontinuation of Antiretroviral Therapy among Adults Receiving HIV Care in the United States" studied why HIV-positive adults sometimes discontinue antiretroviral therapy (ART). Their literature review is a neat, sharply-written paragraph:

> Previous research on ART utilization has focused primarily on adherence.[4 citations] Examinations of the prevalence and predictors of ART discontinuation have demonstrated that certain patients are more likely to discontinue ART. Substance use,[citation] injection drug use,[citation] disease severity,[4 citations] younger age,[3 citations] racial/ethnic minorities,[2 citations] female gender,[2 citations] unemployment,[citation] perceived HIV stigma,[citation] fear of discrimination,[citation] mental health, unemployment,[5 citations] and side effects[citation] have been associated with ART discontinuation. However, these studies lack generalizability since they were conducted on subpopulations of HIV-infected patients, such as patients from 1 or a small group of clinics or hospitals, women only, or patients with a history of substance abuse. There are no population-based estimates of ART discontinuation nor has the distinction between provider-initiated and non–provider-initiated ART discontinuation been examined in previous literature. ART discontinuation and its effects will become an increasingly important issue as patients and providers come to adopt current universal treatment guidelines and the treatment eligible population increases.[12]

Other disciplines are less formally prescriptive. In humanistic fields, the literature review may appear almost anywhere in the opening section. Sometimes the bulk of it will appear in the text, while in other cases it may be consigned to the notes, or some combination of the two.

Tip

When it comes to using secondary sources effectively, think about why you are citing them. If a citation seems obligatory to you (as in, "I know I have to cite critics, so here one is") it will likely come across that way to your reader—and, more important, is unlikely to advance your own thinking.

Two useful metaphors for effective use of secondary sources are building blocks and weaving. If a source helps you build your argument, that is a good thing. Likewise, if you can weave your ideas in with the ideas of others, that is also good. Often, in the course of working up an idea, it will become evident to me that so-and-so is a "must-cite" because her argument dovetails (a third metaphor, I suppose) in some way with my own. When my thinking on a subject is advanced by weaving in what someone else has said, I know I am getting farther than I could on my own.

But perhaps the most effective way to learn how to use secondary sources effectively is to pay attention to how authors you admire build their arguments. When I run across something I think is especially smart, after I have processed the content, I look back at the rhetoric and structure of the argument.

—**CLARE VIRGINIA EBY**

Please don't minimize the work of your predecessors. Without it, you wouldn't be doing yours. Remember that you're explaining, not just critiquing (even if your literature review presents the history of a particular critique). One mark of a nervous writer is the "ritual slaughter of critics" who came before.[13] If everything that everyone ever wrote before is useless, then what makes you so sure that your work isn't useless, too? Your contribution can still have value even if you allow that other people might have written some worthwhile stuff before you. This is also a matter of courtesy. The writers of your sources belong to the community of people who care about your topic. Even if you think you've got a better idea, they're going to be among the more important readers you show it to.

Instead of burying your antecedents, converse with them. You don't need to rehearse that conversation in comprehensive detail—in fact, it's your job not to. You should identify the landmark sources, the ones that have set the terms for the conversation about a subject. To tell your story of who did what before you came along, you should also identify the sources that are most relevant to your own.

Most scholarly work intersects with multiple audiences. Who's going to read your work? Assess the varied needs of your audience as you decide what to emphasize and what to leave out.

Influential sources, and sometimes particular arguments, shape the conversation about a subject over time. The accumulation of information over time is what brings you to your own contribution. Like most parts of an argument, *your literature review is a story, so allow the narrative to emerge.*

That narrative will cut a path through a thicket. Imagine the relevant scholarly discourse on a topic as a bush, with different lines of inquiry (branches, twigs, buds), some crisscrossing, some more grown out than others. Where in the bush are you, the writer? Are you in the thick of familiar questions (thick branches) well inside the bush? (For example, are you taking up familiar questions but answering them in a novel way?) Or are you at the outer edge, at the end of one specific, slender branch (asking a new question)? Are you writing at an unexplored intersection of two branches? To explain where you are, you'll need to describe the bush—but with an emphasis on your place within it.[14]

> ## Furthermore
>
> All writers follow conventions, and there are many of them attached to the literature review. It helps to identify those conventions, not assume them—and that goes for more than literature reviews. If you follow convention blindly, you don a cement jacket within which it's hard to move. But if you make a conscious decision to follow conventional practice (or maybe to follow some practices and not others), you will keep your writerly self mobile and flexible.

In the spirit of this metaphor: Make the conversation with your sources organic, not mechanical. Turn it into a thoughtful engagement, not an empty ritual. To that end, "be more personal," urges Elizabeth Rankin. "When we hear scholars speak about their research" in person, she says, "we learn more than any lit review ever reveals about the sources of inspiration and influence on their work." There's a lesson here: *Make your literature review sound like what it is: a story of how the work of others helped you arrive at your own idea.*

So use the literature review to showcase your perspective alongside those of your predecessors. You're telling your readers about a body of work that people have been adding to since before you arrived at the party. That work necessarily matters to you in some way—so show that it does. Remember that academic writers teach their work, and good teachers animate their material with their own convictions. That includes the literature review.

Create Conclusions, Not Concussions

Many academic writers make a bad choice: they don't conclude. Instead, they simply stop. Just stopping is a habit reinforced during college. It's occasioned by the realization that the writer has just reached the required word length, and now it's time to go to bed. Unless discarded, that habit will continue in graduate school and beyond. When you pound the brakes in this way instead of gliding to a halt, the abrupt stop hurls the reader (the passenger aboard your train of thought) against the seat in front of her. The result is a blow to the head.

Instead, adopt a "conclusive mood." Or, to put it another way, think like an airline pilot who descends gradually and readies the passengers for touchdown. Find your own way of signaling what the pilot says explicitly: that you've begun your descent.

For Example

A section marker with a title like "Expanding the Frame" helps to create such a conclusive mood. Martin L. Johnson, the author of a marker by that name, asks in his conclusion "just what kind of 'local' is present in the local film."

There are various good ways to bring yourself in for a landing. English teachers generally do an execrable job of teaching them to beginning writers. Countless academic writers enter college believing that the job of a conclusion is to robotically repeat what they said in their introduction.

Summing up your argument—rather than just repeating it—is a more sophisticated version of that move, but that, too, is only rarely a good strategy. It only makes sense when you choose it with the reader's welfare in mind. If your argument is especially long or complicated, for example, you may decide that reviewing it at closing will help your reader understand and retain it better. I'm calling this a **Retrospective Conclusion**. Here's an example from an article that studies the impact of a new water supply in Brazil:

> This study indicates that innovative, carefully planned programmes which promote partnerships between Municipalities and communities and which are technically appropriate are critical for their success. The efficiency and sustainability of the family-based water supply system reflects a considerable degree of technical knowledge, managerial know-how and community participation. Variations in water development and water use patterns among households, illustrate the role of socioeconomic level, social networks, managerial practices, water preferences and water sharing. They increased equitability of water use prior to the centralized water system and prevented all households from increasing their consumption afterwards. These factors thus need to be considered by Municipalities in Brazil as they increasingly provide community water supplies and other social services as part of the national decentralization program.[15]

If you choose to conclude by looking backward and summarizing claims you've already made, you should provide the reader with new ways to think about them. That's because even if it turns back to ground you've already covered, *your conclusion needs to do something new.*

The best conclusions look forward. They offer something new to think about. You don't have to make a new argument in your conclusion (and you don't have the space to support one in any case). But you can explore new implications that arise from the argument you just finished. It's usually better to use your conclusion to look forward toward these implications. I call this a **Prospective Conclusion**. Another good name for it is "trumpet conclusion," because it opens outward like a horn and makes noise. Here's Charles Darwin's famous coda to the first edition of *The Origin of Species*:

Thus, from the war of nature, from famine and death, the most exalted object which we are capable of conceiving, namely, the production of higher animals, directly follows. There is grandeur in this view of life, with its several powers, having been originally breathed into a few forms or into one; whilst this planet has gone cycling on according to the fixed law of gravity, from so simple a beginning endless forms most beautiful and wonderful have been, and are being, evolved.[16]

Darwin argued with exceptional care throughout his landmark 1859 book. Nowhere in it does the word "evolution" appear, and only with the book's literal final word ("evolved") does he invoke that explosive idea.

Think of an argument as beginning on the top step of a staircase that others have built before you. You climb their stairs, and then you build your own stairs on top of theirs. You climb your own stairs, and from your top step you see new vistas. These vistas represent new implications for possible future claims that connect to the one that you just made. That's the writer's context for a prospective conclusion.

The contemplation of those vistas marks the moment when you move to conclude. The new implications you see could, in a future piece of writing, turn into a new claim. You might even state this claim in a speculative way—that is, offer a hypothesis that you can support another time. In this way, you can stake out intellectual territory to explore later.

You can also look backward and forward within the same conclusion. You can use a short summation as a segue into a discussion of new implications. Here is the conclusion to a study of hearing loss among hockey referees that combines the retrospective and the prospective:

This pilot study was the first step in evaluating the noise exposure and hearing loss of indoor hockey officials. Preliminary surveys indicate engineering controls are not feasible and officials do not wear hearing protection. Exposure to hazardous levels of noise . . . may increase the risk of permanent hearing loss. Based on the results of this study . . . further research is warranted. Future research should include noise monitoring at a larger venue, audiometric testing in a room with allowable background noise levels, and postgame audiometry within minutes of the game's end. Further research has the potential to identify officials of other sporting events, regionally and nationally, who might be at risk of [noise-induced hearing loss]. In an effort to reduce noise exposure, hockey officials should consider wearing hearing protection while officiating games.[17]

You can see how the writer looks backward and then turns forward to chart a future agenda.

In conclusion (as it were), *be creative when you conclude, and remember that you're not limited to a tired summary*.

And now, on to smaller—but no less important!—elements.

Paragraphs

Paragraphs are basic units of argumentation, the bricks with which you assemble your forensic edifice. A paragraph needs to be sturdy, so that it won't come apart under the pressure of scrutiny. "A paragraph with strong internal organization is a gorgeous thing," wrote a contemporary writing sage.[18] Building one takes skillful attention.

But most paragraphs don't live alone. Building many of them— as you must, to construct an argument—takes planning. Each one must be sensibly shaped to stack atop the paragraph preceding it and to support the one that will follow.

In persuasive scholarly writing, every paragraph has a discernible, coherent structure that centers on a main claim. That claim may have offshoots (or implications). If it's very short, it may have none. The rule is that *the main claim guides the paragraph.*

Your paragraphs hold up your argument. Assemble them with care, for an unsound paragraph can cause damage beyond its own boundaries, especially if it houses a key point.

A Paragraph Is a Story

Like arguments, **paragraphs are stories.** Like good arguments, good paragraphs exhibit a this-follows-that narrative logic. A typical paragraph has a beginning, middle, and end—but to bring them into view, you need to figure out the story your paragraph is telling. You may have to move sentences around to figure out which ones belong where. That activity is made clearest by example, so here's an exercise. How would you order these four sentences?

> The clabber that results from the churning of butter is remarkable for its tang. After you've mixed the wet and dry ingredients together, banana bread should be baked thoroughly. The secret ingredient is buttermilk. Don't overmix the batter.

You probably noticed is that these four sentences don't make a complete paragraph by themselves. After you reorder the sentences, you'll have to write more of them—and you'll likely have to tinker with some of the original ones to make them fit. *If you can complete this exercise, that's because you could already see the story that the paragraph is trying to tell.* That shows the power of narrative as an organizing principle. When you reassemble the fragments, you could wind up with something like this:

> The clabber, or buttermilk, that results from the churning of butter is remarkable for its tang. It's the secret ingredient of Rififi banana bread. The quick and delicious recipe in the *Cheesequake Gazette* warns that after you've mixed the wet and dry ingredients together, you shouldn't overmix the batter. Banana bread should be baked thoroughly.

This exercise shows how we automatically want to assemble and complete a story, even a scrambled one. But a paragraph is much easier to read if it tells a discernible story that asserts and develops its claim in the first place.

Organize and sequence the sentences in each paragraph so that the reader can follow where it's going. Disorganized paragraphs give the reader a headache. The pain comes on because the reader will have to unscramble your thoughts, as in the exercise I set up earlier. Sometimes the reader won't succeed in reordering the ideas in a messy paragraph. Whether she does or not, after too many such paragraphs, she'll give up and step off your train of thought.

Clear topic sentences will anchor your paragraphs. Topic sentences are small-scale signposts: they tell your reader what's coming in the next few sentences. If you bury them, your reader will have to orient herself in a moving current of ideas.

Try This

When you skim a piece of academic writing, you will often find yourself leaping from topic sentence to topic sentence, as you might stones in a brook. This readerly practice shows how important it is to write clear, declarative topic sentences.

To test your own, **line up the topic sentences of all of your paragraphs in order.** Taken together, the topic sentences that make up the body of your writing should form a clear and flowing précis of your argument. If they don't, the gaps or digressions should be plain to see.

It follows that you can only write a good topic sentence if you know what's coming yourself. You have to organize your thoughts. Sometimes you'll write a paragraph and then have to unscramble it. (I moved many sentences around to create the paragraphs in this section.) Or you may find that you just wrote your way to the point you want to make. In that event, you will have written an upside-down paragraph.

Beware of Upside-Down Paragraphs

When you write a paragraph of this type (and we all do), realize what it signifies so that you can take appropriate measures. On the one hand, an upside-down paragraph is an example of induction: working your way toward a reveal of the main idea. But that's true only if you plan it that way. Most often, upside-down paragraphs are a symptom of half-baked writing. The ingredients may be delicious, but they need more preparation.

If you find yourself writing your way to an idea, remember the old writer's saying *"I write to find out what I think"* and its sequel *"Then I begin."* Take your final idea from that upside-down paragraph and start over again. This writer would have benefited from doing that:

> Let us look at the title of the foundational text of Chinese philosophy, which the above-mentioned work by the French Sinologist is about, the Yi Jing. Consisting of sixty-four hexagrams based on a complex multiplication of the two cosmic propensities of yinyang, Yi Jing attempts to represent cosmic phenomena and their constancy and mutations. The tension and correlation between yin and yang is captured in the title of the book, 易經 (Yi Jing). Often translated as "Book of Changes," Yi Jing could be more accurately translated as the "Unchangeable Script of (Non-)changeability." While 經 (jing) etymologically means "the warp", that is, the unchangeable line of weaving, 易 (yi) connotes at once effortlessness (簡易), changeability (變異), and nonchangeability or invariability (不易).4 Yi Jing as unchangeable scripture of (non-)changeability is made possible by the dynamic correlation of yinyang: while yang ascends and vaporizes, yin descends and concretizes, yin's propensity for

rigidity and stillness is equally as forceful as yang's propensity for flexibility and mutation. In light of this, I argue that while it is necessary to critique the Orientalist "denial of coevalness," it is at best only a partial "decolonization." The critique should not automatically overlook the (possibility of) unchanging relevance or "haunting" of a concept from the past in the present. Yinyang still matters in contemporary China, despite and because of its long history of mutation.[19]

If this paragraph had started where it now ends, it would have been easier to read. ***To fix an upside-down paragraph, imagine yourself reaching into the paragraph to grab the main idea, and then pulling it inside-out by extracting that main idea and placing it first.*** On a related note:

Don't Bury Your Topic Sentences

If you shove a rightful topic sentence into a pile of other sentences, your reader will have to orient herself in a moving current of ideas. Instead, use them as small-scale signposts: they tell your reader what's coming in the next few sentences.

The beginnings of paragraphs present you with an unmatched opportunity to shape your reader's experience. As an academic writer, you should grab this opportunity to make strong analytical claims. Don't fill the topic-sentence space with mushy descriptive claims like this one:

> In Creedence Clearwater Revival's "Looking Out My Back Door," John Fogerty sings of rural nature.

That may be true, but it just describes the song. A paragraph starting with this sentence still has to find its way to an interesting and challenging claim. On the other hand, this sentence starts out with one:

In "Looking Out My Back Door," John Fogerty gives quiet urgency to a pastoral vision that evolved from Creedence Clearwater Revival's earliest music.

For Example

Misplaced topic sentences are close cousins to upside-down paragraphs. For example:

> While Chandler distances himself from Oscar Wilde's more virulent persecutors, he maintains the belief that homosexuals are impossible for non-homosexuals to empathize with, except through repulsion by proxy. Nevertheless, we should also note that Chandler's smug bemusement at the idea of homosexuality—a blend of pity, tolerance, and disgust—shows that his interest in the topic was genuine, at least as a means to understand "normal" human nature. Alongside his opinion that he could not "take the homo seriously as a moral outcast" he believed that "there aught [*sic*] to be a good novel in homosexualism." **Above all, it is most important to note how Chandler's views on homosexuality are bound up with his feelings about writing, and artistic merit.** He saw potential in what he saw as the "surface brilliance" of the Wildean mode, but also saw it as fundamentally shallow, hollow, and immature.

When you move the bolded sentence to the top, everything suddenly makes more sense.

This analytical claim invites the development of a larger argument. The paragraph that follows will be more complicated—and also more compelling—because it begins with a prospective analysis.

Assert your ideas and develop them. An argument that begins with an analytical claim will include descriptive claims as support, but it won't be guided by them. Fresh topic sentences will advance your argument and allow you to set the terms by which you introduce your evidence.

A crisp paragraph starts with a claim. Then it supports and elaborates on that claim—and gets ready for the next claim that will come in the next paragraph. Meandering paragraphs fail to do these things. Most often, they contain multiple claims. When you take a meandering paragraph apart, it will often contain a collection of topic sentences. It follows that the claims made by these sentences won't be developed. As you revise, some or all of them may become the nuclei of their own paragraphs—and some will likely prove unnecessary.

Don't End a Paragraph with a Block Quotation

I've said that whenever you quote, you hand the microphone to someone else. Their voice will take center stage instead of yours. For that reason, I suggested in chapter 1 that you limit your use of quotations, period. Still, we all need to quote sometimes: you need to acknowledge relevant sources and competing arguments. But not all times are equal.

When you end a paragraph with a block quotation, you surrender your voice at the point when you should most want it: when you're coming to a conclusion. This is *your* piece of writing; don't give this valuable space to someone else.

Even if the quotation isn't a block quotation, it still gives away your voice at the moment when you sum up your argument or claim in some way—which is when the reader is most keen to hear what *you* think. *The quoted writer has to carry your water, not the other way around.* The one exception: if the quotation is just a few words and you're folding it into one of your own sentences:

We may say, then, that the flipped classroom exemplifies Henry David Thoreau's ideal of a government that "governs least," and therefore "governs best."

The aphorism here may be Thoreau's, but the sentence still belongs to the writer, who harnesses its wit.

The Geometry of Paragraphs

Like essays, paragraphs typically contain arguments. Some may even read like essays in microcosm. A good paragraph develops a main idea and advances it. These ideas necessarily subordinate themselves to the larger argument of which they are parts. (That is, paragraphs together assemble a larger unit of meaning: the argument as a whole.) But paragraphs are also units of meaning on their own.

The same triangular geometry I used to describe arguments applies to paragraphs too—but less sternly. I've advised against inductive arguments in academic writing because when you write toward your main point, you may frustrate the academic reader, who wants to know what you're up to sooner rather than later. Deductive arguments—when you write *from* your main point—show the reader that point sooner, which is especially valuable if your argument is complex. Deduction better fits the academic reader's specific needs most of the time.

But paragraphs are shorter than essays or books, and so afford more flexibility. An inductive paragraph here or there isn't going to strain the reader, and will provide useful variety to enliven the reading experience. (You also need to vary your sentence structure for the same reason; I'll have more to say about that in a moment.)

You can imagine paragraphs as well-balanced pyramids that can stand on either the base or the point. A paragraph that moves from point to base—that is, deductively—starts with a specific analytical claim ("Emma Goldman was a provocateur as a matter of personality") and broadens outward to a wide base of supporting detail, which might show how Goldman's provocations were national and international, public and private. Or it might move in a different direction to show how Goldman provoked people long before she turned activist. That structure looks like this:

Here's an example of a deductively structured paragraph:

> Probably no form of essentializing music is as widespread as *notation*. Notation represents oral traditions or the composer's intent or the publishing industry's commodity, and therefore it exhibits remarkably diverse capabilities of disciplining music. Notation insists on the music's right to be just what it is, black on white, notes on the page, music as object. Notation removes music from the time and space that it occupies through performance, thereby decontextualizing it. Choices about notation usually detextualize it as well, for example by unraveling 'the music's' relation with other texts, the myth of Javanese *wayang* or the political novel or dramatic piece that provides the libretto to the nineteenth-century opera.[20]

The author opens with a clear claim about notation and then elaborates it outward. Each succeeding point refers back to the initial assertion.

An inductive paragraph that moves from base to point—an upside-down pyramid—might begin with a broad descriptive statement ("People needed paper to write on, and also for hygiene (toilet paper), commerce (money), and religion—among other things"). That statement might give way to further supporting description before it narrows to a pointed statement: "We may therefore say that paper was the technology that drove modernity." An inductive paragraph looks like this:

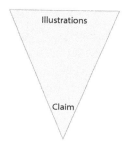

Here's a published example:

Such hostile working conditions and general poverty, in combination with high unemployment and ongoing political violence, have resulted in a dismal work environment for Guatemalans in general and Maya in particular. Indeed, little with regard to the economy and labor conditions appears to have changed for the better since Bossen conducted research in the 1970s and 1980s. We would be remiss, however, in limiting our analysis to broad statistical data.[21]

This inductive example moves from concrete details to a broader, abstract statement about the need to move beyond statistics. Conversely, the deductive example moves from the abstract to the concrete. These progressions (abstract → concrete; or concrete → abstract) emerge because the concrete and the abstract need each other if the author wants to create meaning that the reader can follow. I'll talk further about the necessary bond between abstract and the concrete in chapter 3.

Some paragraphs take the shape of rectangles. Unlike triangular paragraphs, these rectangles don't contain fully-formed and supported main points of their own. This unusual kind of paragraph invariably appears in the middle of a longer explanation of something, as part of a larger group of paragraphs that together make a larger point. For example, here are two consecutive rectangular paragraphs:

In the four centuries of that triangular trade, ten to eleven million people—fifty or sixty thousand a year in the peak decades between 1700 and 1850—were packed beneath slave ship decks and sent to the New World. Indeed, up to the year 1820, five times as many Africans traveled across the Atlantic as did Europeans. And those numbers do not include the dead—the five percent of the human cargo who died in crossings that took three weeks, the quarter who died in crossings that took three months. Behind the numbers lie the horrors of the Middle Passage: chained slaves forced to dance themselves into shape on the decks; the closed holds, where men and women were separated from one another and chained into the space of a coffin; the stifling heat and untreated illness; the suicides and slave revolts, the dead thrown overboard as the ships passed on.

The United States Constitution, ratified in 1789, contained a provision that led to a ban on the importation of African slaves after 1808. Closing the trade was favorable to both opponents of slavery and a portion of slaveholders, mostly Virginians, who feared that the continued importation of slaves would dilute the social power that their own slaves supported. . . . In the seven decades between the Constitution and the Civil War, approximately one million enslaved people were relocated from the upper South to the lower South according to the dictates of the slaveholders' economy, two thirds of these through a pattern of commerce that soon became institutionalized as the domestic slave trade.[22]

These paragraphs collect evidence without moving to or from a main point within their own boundaries. They form part of a larger layout of evidence that the author has broken up into paragraphs to allow the reader's eye to glide more easily through it. A rectangular paragraph doesn't have independent existence in that it doesn't showcase its own developed point. Instead, it's part of a series of paragraphs that together support a larger argument that is explicitly articulated elsewhere. The author here advances the story through description—that is, context. This background enables him to make further analytical claims later on.

Most of your paragraphs should be triangular—which is to say that they should have a main point that you develop and support. *But a rectangular paragraph offers a way to break up a longer discussion.* Like most sound writerly judgments, rectangular paragraphs arise from a concern for the reader's welfare. Without them, a paragraph might last for a page or more, which tires your reader. This brings me to paragraphs that aren't tiring at all:

In Praise of Short Paragraphs

Sometimes a very short paragraph will be in order. Many academic writers think that short paragraphs are frivolous. They reek of (gasp) journalism, the refuge of superficial minds. Short paragraphs, it is said, show a reduced attention span on the part of the writer. As such, they bespeak a lack of serious purpose, and casual writerly execution.

Not so. Short paragraphs have force.

Their isolation in white space stands out and allows you to make important points that stand out because they stand alone. Used judiciously, short paragraphs give power to your exposition. They allow you to create more complicated rhythms than if you simply place one thick brick of text atop another, and they give zing to your voice at the times when you need it. In short, they're another tool in a good writer's kit.

Furthermore

"You just said that a paragraph is a story," I hear you point out. So you may ask, "How can a one- or two-sentence paragraph be a story?"

The answer is that it can be a very short story. The most famous work of what is now called "flash fiction" runs just six words:

For sale: baby shoes, never worn.

(This story has been attributed to Ernest Hemingway, but there's good evidence that he had nothing to do with it.)

Short paragraphs tell short stories.

Furthermore

The same principle of brevity applies to chapters. Before you write an eighty-page chapter, stop and ask yourself a question: Why write something you wouldn't want to read yourself?

Transitions between Paragraphs

Because paragraphs work together to form arguments, they have to connect. Think of paragraphs in sequence, then, because they rarely stand alone. Those sequences form sections. The sections form the larger argument. As the sage said, *Academic writers must teach their paragraphs to know each other.*[23] *That's a poetic way of saying that you must create functional transitions between them.*

The simplest transitions result from the use of what Richard Marius calls "transactional words." Such words—"therefore," "however," "nevertheless," et al.—signal the reader that you're pivoting from one part of your argument to another. They also signal the direction of the pivot. Transactional words are useful tools, then. You're probably accustomed to using them already.[24]

> **Tip**
>
> If you're writing something long, like a thesis, dissertation, or monograph, imagine that the reader will come to the chapters at one-month intervals. This is a rule of thumb that will remind you to **repeat your key points (the through-line of your argument) from chapter to chapter** without having to fully elaborate them each time.

Another reliable transition is to repeat a word or phrase from the end of one paragraph near the beginning of the next. With the repetition of the word "transition," I used this technique to move from the first to the second paragraph of this section. Here's an example from a well-known sociological study by Erving Goffman:

> Those who come together into a sub-community or milieu may be called *social deviants*, and their corporate life a deviant community. They constitute a special type, but only one type, of deviator.
>
> If there is to be a field of inquiry called "deviance," it is social deviants as here defined that would presumably constitute its core.[25]

Goffman uses variations on the word "deviate" to execute his transition between paragraphs. This strategy maintains the writer's point of view.

The possibilities for transitions in written English exceed these—they're myriad—but the best ones are enabled by logic. If the structure of your argument makes logical sense, you'll find it easier to formulate transitions among its small and large parts. If you encounter repeated trouble doing so, that's a signal that you should reconsider your organization scheme.

Sentences

Others have written about the aesthetics of sentences. I will stage no such beauty pageant. Not every sentence you write has to be gorgeous. You can write well even if none of them are. But your sentences have to do their job—and that job is my focus here.

Paragraphs are the larger bricks that build arguments. Sentences are the smaller bricks that build paragraphs. A poorly formed brick can destabilize the larger structure. This sentence will make the edifice wobble:

> Although the project of rethinking these foundational oppositions and their pervasive intellectual effects is now widespread in social and literary theory, I discuss these developments from a much narrower perspective.[26]

Here's a rewritten version that highlights the important statement that the author is making in the first clause and sets up a clearer "they say/I say":

> In social and literary theory, the project of rethinking these foundational oppositions and their pervasive intellectual effects is now widespread. However, I discuss these developments from a much narrower perspective.

The revised version doesn't add or subtract meaning from the original, or even change any phrases. Instead, it alters the reveal of information to make it easier to understand quickly.

The following stemwinding sentence relies heavily on obscure abstractions that the reader is presumed to be familiar with already:

> But Marcuse's negotiation of Lukács's formative theory of reification is also more complex than the Frankfurt Schools' reframing of reification tends to suggest: in his early work, the concept carries the insidious, mystifying implications it carried in Lukács—the reification to be triumphed over—as well as more positive, liberatory, erotic implications—the reification to be suffered through as a means to this triumph.[27]

So deeply is the writer wrapped in his own formulations here (look at all the dashes!) that I can't rewrite or paraphrase the sentence at all.

Like your paragraphs, your sentences have to be clear, both on their own and in relation to one another, so that you can stack them into something bigger and more complex. Like paragraphs, sentences cohabit with other sentences, so they have to know each other. *Each sentence needs to show an awareness of where it came from, and point to where you're going next.*

Here is a cluster of ringingly clear sentences that link to each other to illustrate a tension in identity theory. The author, Kwame Anthony Appiah, moves back and forth between the abstract and the concrete to create a harmonious balance. (I'll say more about the essential value of the abstract–concrete balance in the next chapter.)

> Suppose, for example, I adopt a lifestyle as a solitary traveler around the world, free of entanglements with family and community, settling for a few months here and there, making what little money I need by giving English lessons to businesspeople. My parents tell me that I am wasting my life as a Scholar Gypsy, that I have a good education, talent as a musician, and a wonderful gift for friendship, all of which are being put to no use. You don't have to be a communitarian to wonder whether

it is a satisfactory response to say only that I have considered the options and this is the way I have chosen. Don't I need to say something about what this way makes possible for me and for those I meet? Or about what other talents of mine it makes use of? It is one thing to say that the government or society or your parents ought not to stop you from wasting your life if you choose to; but it is another to say that wasting your life in your own way is good just because it *is* your way, just because you have chosen to waste your life.[28]

In this inductively-structured passage, Appiah gradually uncovers a tension between living for oneself or for others.

In her discussion of the deficient leadership of President Andrew Johnson, Annette Gordon-Reed creates a similar unity through the artful use of metaphor:

Now, of course, those who are afraid to be wrong are afraid to be right, because leadership and decision making inevitably contain an element of risk. So, in a time that required that overused but very useful and descriptive modern phrase "thinking outside the box," [President Andrew] Johnson was inside a box with the lid shut tight. In the aftermath of a fratricidal war and the destruction of the South's slavery-based economic system, America needed forward thinking—flexible, practical, yet visionary leadership. Lincoln had spoken of a "new birth of freedom" at Gettysburg as he sought to extend the meaning of Jefferson's Declaration of Independence to cover what he knew would be the altered circumstances of the post–Civil War United States. The country had been broken and could not be put back together in precisely the same form as existed before. Johnson, on the other hand, looked resolutely backward.[29]

Gordon-Reed takes a cliché ("thinking outside the box") and makes it her own by giving it an original turn. Then she uses a forward/backward image to organize her contrast between Abraham Lincoln and his successor.

Tip
On semicolons

Semicolons link main clauses—that is, phrases that can stand alone as grammatically correct sentences. When you link two clauses by a semicolon, you assert a connection between them that must be understandable without further explanation.

Semicolons create longer and more complex sentences that ask more from a reader. You should therefore use them sparingly.

Treat semicolons like cherry cordials: don't overindulge. Limit yourself to no more than one per page.

Don't Be Afraid to Write Simple Sentences

Sentences need clarity to convey their direction. Short sentences with simple subject-verb structures are clear, and also direct. This straightforward example adds a welcome dollop of wit:

> At its simplest, capitalism is an activity—it is the accumulation of, well, capital.[30]

Academic writers who avoid simple sentences produce tangled paragraphs that the reader must hack through with an interpretive machete in order to expose their main points. Such work takes more than patience; it also exhausts the reader's stamina. The following sentence is clear enough, but irritatingly hard to get through because it pays scant attention to the reader running alongside, gasping for breath:

Since the elimination of differences project is fundamentally impossible in a world of blurred boundaries, mixed marriages, shared languages, and other deep connectivities, it is bound to produce an order of frustration that can begin to account for the systematic excess that we see in today's headlines.[31]

Remember what Pete Seeger said in praise of Woody Guthrie: "Any damn fool can get complicated. It takes genius to attain simplicity."[32]

Vary Your Sentence Structure

Your writing will sound better, and will therefore be more interesting to read, if you vary the structure of your sentences. You might include a dependent clause, as in this sentence, which opens with one:

Because the term *white crime* lacks social meaning, the term *white criminal* is also perplexing.[33]

When you add more than one dependent clause, a sentence gets complex. This one, by the same author, has two:

Many people are unaware that, although minstrel shows were plainly designed to pander to white racism and to make whites feel comfortable with—indeed, entertained by—racial oppression, African Americans formed a large part of the black minstrels' audience.[34]

The main idea conveyed by this sentence is that many African American people watched minstrel shows even though they were aimed at white audiences. In this case, the author inserts a dependent clause ("although . . .") along the way, and then another ("indeed, entertained by") into that one. This extra information enriches the main idea, but the author risks that the two detours may cause the reader to get lost. I think she gets away with it in this instance, and reaps a larger payoff.

Furthermore

You can write a run-on sentence if you show elsewhere that you know what you're doing—and if the run-on offers you a chance to say what you want to say in the best way. Stephen Greenblatt serves up a very long one here:

> These three sentences manifest the blank refusal of logical connectives characteristic of much of early travel writing, but there is a hidden logic: Cartier's reading of the natives' response to barter has led him to the conclusion that they would be easy to convert; the task of conversion will necessitate the learning of their language, which here begins with the notation of their words for two of the European articles in which they take such delight; and the inscription of Indian words in European letters is paradoxically a step toward the renaming, the linguistic appropriation of, the land.

Interpreting an early work of travel writing, Greenblatt wants to spotlight a logical sequence within a passage, so he unspools that sequence in a series of main clauses that he joins by semicolons. This sentence breaks a lot of rules, but no matter: its nimbleness shows Greenblatt's command of his story. Recall the first rule of good writing: You can do anything as long as it works.

On Recursion

These more complicated sentence structures exemplify recursion, which refers to the embedding of clauses within sentences. Recursion is part of what makes language sound human, as opposed to a robotic string of subject-verb sentences. Many linguists believe recursion to be common to all human language.

I've said that an argument is a story, and that a paragraph is a story. Not every sentence is a story, but thanks to recursion, some are. This one by Garrison Keillor always makes me smile:

> A hard frost hits in September, sometimes as early as Labor Day, and kills the tomatoes that we, being frugal, protected with straw and paper tents, which we, being sick of tomatoes, left some holes in.[35]

Katharine and E. B. White caution that dissecting humor can kill it, but let's take a chance.* Keillor's sentence conveys a whole story, complete with a surprise ending. That ending is enabled by recursion: the dependent clauses advance the narrative, and the last nested pair of them ("which we, being sick of tomatoes, left some holes in") invert it.

Embrace recursion by all means. Recursion will bring grace and gratifying variety to your writing. But be careful with it, too. Unless you are the second coming of William Faulkner, too much recursion will risk stuffing your sentences until they burst, like this:

> The sky was, thanks to its cerulean refraction, observed by the monks of Bologna (whose medieval gardens awed the pope), blue.[36]

Limit recursion in your topic sentences in particular, for two reasons:

1) Recursion inhibits skimming, which is essential to the scholarly enterprise.

---

* "Humor can be dissected, as a frog can," wrote the Whites in 1941, "but the thing dies in the process and the innards are discouraging to any but the purely scientific mind." E. B. White and Katharine S. White, "The Preaching Humorist," *Saturday Review of Literature*, October 18, 1941, 16+, at 16.

2) Recursion slows the reader's entry into a paragraph, delaying comprehension, increasing tension and ambiguity (how will this sentence end?) at a point when the reader ordinarily does not want tension—which I am deliberately creating by extending the ending of this sentence past the point where the reader wants it to stop already.

Begin most sentences—not just topic sentences—with the subject. This practice will make it easier for use-driven readers to follow you. (Good topic sentences help a skimming reader.) But don't begin all of your sentences that way, or else you'll sound like an Ernest Hemingway parody. Add some variety. Therefore:

Get Rhythm

Try to alternate short sentences with longer ones to create a rhythm. This good example starts with a simple declarative sentence that makes it easy for the reader to ease into the more complex sentence that follows:

> What Google couldn't build, it bought. In 2013 the corporation won a reported bidding war with Facebook for Israeli social mapping startup Waze, a firm that pioneered community-sourced real-time traffic information.[37]

But don't alternate in a rigid back-and-forth way (short/long/short/long, etc.). That's monotony, not rhythm. Rhythms worth listening to are more variable than that. These sentences establish a satisfyingly complex cadence:

> T.S. Eliot wrote Groucho Marx a fan letter in 1961, requesting a photograph of the comic actor and humorist. Groucho enthusiastically complied, sending a photograph of himself out of character, sans bushy eyebrows, glasses, and cigar, and the two continued corresponding until they finally met in June 1964, in London, when Groucho and his third wife, Eden, went to

the Eliots' house for dinner. Eliot never gave a public account of what transpired that evening. Groucho, though, described the occasion in a letter written the following day to his brother Gummo.[38]

Listen to your writing. (When you can, read it aloud.) If you vary your sentence structure to create a flowing rhythm, the reader will sense that rhythm through both sight and sound.

Citations

When and How to Cite

I begin with a tricolon:

> *If you need a source's exact words, quote them in the text.*
> *If you need the source's ideas, paraphrase them in the text.*
> *If you need neither, but want only to show that you've read the source as part of your own research, then place the source's name and work in a footnote or endnote (or a parenthetical citation).*

The underlying principle here: quote only when you need to, and not when you don't. The reason: because *as much as possible, your writing should speak in your own voice, and in your own words.*

What Should You Cite?

Facts that are common knowledge don't need citations, but you should provide them for obscure or uncommon knowledge. How do you tell the difference?

Rule of thumb: if you can find a fact in three separate places, then it may be considered common knowledge and need not be cited. (The same goes for a well-known opinion, such as "Golden retrievers are among the friendliest dogs.") A statistic like the coal tonnage mined by Bolivia in 1974 doesn't "belong" to anyone, but you probably won't be able to find it in three places—so you should note the place you do find it.

The guiding logic for these judgments ought to be familiar by now: Think of the reader's needs. If the reader is inspired by your writing and wants to use or respond to it, you need to make the reader's work easier by showing where you got your information.

> **Furthermore**
>
> How much to cite may depend on your field. Legal scholarship, for example, conventionally requires large numbers of citations. But the general rule still applies: Cite what you need to cite to meet the reader's needs.

Footnotes or Endnotes?

You won't always have a choice. Most publications have a preferred house style. So do most teachers. But you can imagine that you have a choice—and you should do that because it will aid your judgment.

While you're writing, imagine all of your citations as endnotes, not footnotes. I'm not implying that endnotes are more correct than footnotes; they're not. Instead, I'm suggesting that your writing will benefit if you imagine your notes at a far remove from the reader's immediate field of vision. You can read a footnote by dropping your gaze downward and barely missing a beat.* For that reason, it's easy—too easy—to think of footnotes as part of the

---

* See what I mean? But now you have to find your place again.

body of your essay or chapter. They can make a writer lazy, the way a motorcyclist might rely on an attached sidecar for balance instead of centering her weight atop the bike.*

Tip

When you're composing, ***treat endnotes like Death Row***. You send stuff to the notes when it looks as if you won't need it. Sometimes it'll stay there, but as you revise and tighten up your writing, you may shuffle some of your notes off the digital coil into the trash bin.

To read an endnote, you have to flip or click to the end of the piece, which is more cumbersome than the simple eye-lowering afforded by a footnote.[39] Fewer readers will bother to check endnotes, so you should think of them as containing information that the reader probably will not see. If you later decide that your argument requires that information, you can lift it into your main text. This brief thought experiment shows that thinking of your references at an endnote's distance away will clarify the judgments you need to make about them. As a result, you'll depend on them less and focus on your argument more. So will your reader.

---

* Overreliance on footnotes can also create confusion for writer and reader alike. Neurologist Oliver Sacks, a superb writer, envisioned footnotes as a challenging, bewildering array. "I am somewhat tormented by the linearity of writing in a book," he said in an interview. "It would be nice if I could present a globe, with plumb lines dropping from every place, which is partly why I like footnotes. Kate [Edgar, Sacks's assistant and frequent collaborator] has to restrain me from writing footnotes to footnotes." *Barnes and Noble Review*, October 26, 2010, https://www.barnesandnoble.com/review /oliver-sacks.

Furthermore

As I am implying here, footnotes aren't for beginners. More than endnotes, they can distract both reader and writer from the needs of argument.

But hyperlinks are downright dangerous. Most writing these days (commercially published or not) never appears on a printed page. So most writers have to confront hyperlinks at some point. Moreover, if you refer to born-digital writing, you can only cite it with a link—which turns into a hyperlink if your writing is read online.

The peril of hyperlinks lies in their ability to convey the reader not just to a potentially—but only briefly—distracting footnote, but to an entirely different piece of writing that lies in a completely different place. A hyperlink is like a *Star Trek* transporter that beams your reader from Chicago to Cancun at a click. Your reader may find Cancun interesting—or another click might send her from there to Canberra. Canberra might prove less compelling, but by then, it would take a very careful and conscientious reader to navigate back to Chicago, where the journey began.

Because hyperlinks extend a literal invitation to read someone else's writing, make your own writing worth returning to.

What are notes for, anyway? Let's first dispense with the obvious: you need notes to document your quotations and direct references (unless you're already doing that in parentheses in your text, as in MLA style). All academic writing requires that information, and the notes are often the place for your citations.

Now let's venture beyond the obvious. Why bother citing anything other than direct references or quotations? It has often been said (by me, in this book) that good writing entails a series of judgment calls. This is one of them. Notes provide extra information that may be relevant, but not directly relevant. When is it worth it to ask the reader to direct attention away from the main path of your argument? With practice, most academic writers develop a feel for when to drop a note.

Rule of thumb: *If a bit of information doesn't advance your argument, you should export it from your main text.* You can choose to delete it, and that will often be for the best. But maybe the information is relevant for some other reason. Perhaps it provides extra—but not strictly necessary—proof of a point you're making. Or maybe you just find it interesting, and you think your reader will too ("He was the stepfather and teacher of a famous juggler, Anthony Gatto"). For such tidbits, academic writers have the luxury of notes.

But remember that aboard your train of thought, your argument always travels first-class. Think of the notes as a second-class compartment. Thus, this rule:

If you can imagine putting "by the way" in front of a phrase, it belongs in your notes.

The Basics of Visual Storytelling

Most of us have some experience reading visual presentations, but it's becoming increasingly necessary to write with them, too.

I spoke in chapter 1 about how metaphors can generate vivid, piercing mental images that teach. Sometimes, though, the best kind of picture is an actual picture. Consider this brief passage from a well-known writer:

> With this kind of treatment, most ovarian cancer patients at her stage survive two years and a third survive five years. About 20 percent of patients are actually cured.[40]

These sentences made me pause for a few beats because the percentages ("most ovarian cancer patients" = at least 51 percent; "a third" = 33 percent; and "about 20 percent") add up to more than 100 percent. I then realized that the first and second categories actually overlap.

It would have been simpler to present the data visually in this case, and others like it. Such visual presentation of information—using charts, graphs, diagrams, and the like—is a form of academic writing. Using images to make arguments is now called "data visualization."* It's an important skill for your toolkit, and more and more academic disciplines require knowledge of it.[41] That knowledge isn't far away, for an ordinary word processing program now provides access to a world of graphic design that was once the exclusive province of technical experts.

Like all academic writing, the visual presentation of data is a form of storytelling. This brief section introduces its foundational concepts.[42]

Consider this story:

The 2012 Republican Party presidential primaries showed Mitt Romney's endurance. Romney gained a solid base of support well in advance of the primary caucuses and elections (which began in January). He then fended off repeated challenges, as one rival after another rose from the ranks to challenge the front-runner, and then fell back. Romney didn't always lead the polls, but he was able to maintain his base of support throughout. As his challengers briefly rose, flagged, and then dropped out of the race, Romney gained many of their voters and consolidated his position. By spring of 2012, he had the support of more than half of the primary electorate, and his nomination became inevitable.

---

* Drawing inferences from data is part of the popular growing field now called data science. That skill lies outside the ambit of this book. But once you've made those inferences and you want to communicate them through data visualization—well, that's just what you would do in any other field. The only difference between old-fashioned prose and data visualization is the latter's use of pictures.

This re-creation of data gathered by RealClear Politics (and inspired by an illustration by David Byler) tells the same story, but more sharply:

Republican Primary Polls, 2012

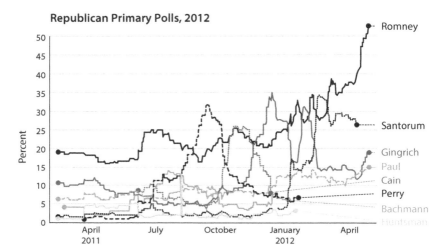

This visual story presented by Byler needs few words to accompany it, and actually conveys more information than my summary does (including the names of Romney's challengers).[43]

Good visuals aren't all that different from the prose writing that is my main subject. Visual storytelling just uses different tools. As a result, many of the do's and don't's of verbal storytelling also apply to the kind that relies on images. The parallel should not surprise anyone. Statistics is a form of rhetoric, and visuals are part of that rhetoric. Here are four rules of visual rhetoric:

Don't Do Anything Too Cute

Present your data accurately and cleanly. The simplest display is usually best. Usually that will mean the basics, such as a scatterplot or a histogram.

Here's a good example of a basic scatterplot:

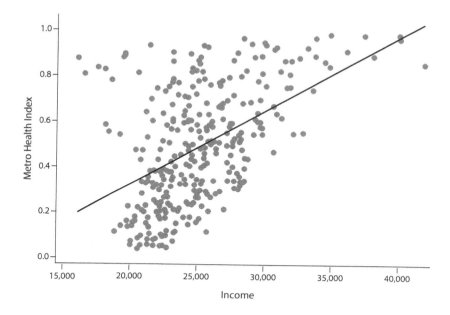

The diagram, drawn from an essay titled "Why Some Cities Are Healthier than Others," plots a city's "Metro Health Index" (the percentage of people who smoke or are obese) and compares it to the city's median income.[44] The scatterplot shows that lower-median income of a city's residents correlates with a higher percentage of smokers or people with obesity. That doesn't mean that one causes the other. It would take a different kind of study to determine whether that's true. But the wide scatter of the data suggests that the correlation is not terribly strong—meaning that many points lie far outside the correlation line that runs through the scatter. If you were shown only the correlation line, you might miss something important. This is an honest presentation, but it also shows the value of the adage "show me the data."

The following visual is a histogram—that is, a graph that tracks the distribution of one variable. This one looks at money.[45] It might arise from a research question like "Is the much-discussed 'top 1 percent' a good marker of wealth inequality in the United States, or just a talking point that went viral?"

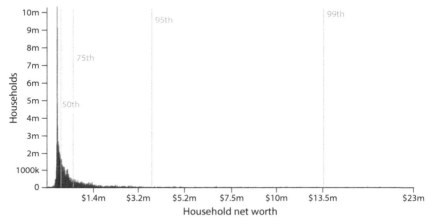

Distribution of Net Worth by Households

A diagram like this can illustrate many possible arguments on the subject. This one has considerable virtues. Most important, it clearly pictures just how rich the top 1 percent are—which we see through the length of the tail that extends along the x-axis.

But this histogram also has some problems in the details. Details matter, so let's consider some of them. Most important, the numbers of households that fall between approximately the 90th and 99th percentiles are so small that they disappear into the x-axis until they're almost invisible. (It would be helpful to create an inset graph to magnify them.) The author adds a useful note about the ultra-rich and how they had to be lumped at the final bar lest they skew the entire chart. The necessity of such a note illustrates certain limits of the visual presentation of data. To depict that group of ultra-rich households, it would be best to generate another chart, perhaps one with a different scale.

Also, the y-axis is marked off at million-unit intervals, so why is the first interval labeled "1000k" (which is a million, but presented in a potentially confusing way)? The creator of the graph also inserts several percentile markers (light gray vertical lines through the middle of the graph). However, the 50th and 75th percentile markers overlap, which is potentially confusing, and also looks bad. The simple solution would be to vary the height of the vertical bars so that the labels don't interfere with each other. Additional vertical bars marking the 96th, 97th, and 98th percentiles would also have helped the viewer—and there's already enough space to include them. The horizontal (x-) axis is also oddly divided, and not drawn to scale. Also, there's no apparent reason to use unusual intervals where a standard 1, 2, 3, 4, 5 . . . would be easier to read.

Even with these flaws, this simple chart still delivers insight. It shows that wealth is indeed highly concentrated, and the amount of wealth at the right of the chart suggests a possible difference between "comfortably" and "powerfully" rich. The top 1 percent is not a bad delimiter, then, but you could make an argument for an even narrower category.

This example shows that you can accomplish a lot with a simple tool. Break out fancy tools—such as 3D diagrams—only when you need to do something fancy (i.e., difficult or complex) that specifically demands those tools. When you write prose, you need to choose the words that communicate your ideas most precisely. When you use visuals, be likewise precise: let your purpose choose the presentation. Don't twist your story so that you can be sure to include the nifty picture that took you three hours to create. *The visuals should serve your ideas, not the other way around.*

When you use visuals, you are teaching the reader—just as you do with words. If you don't start with simple ones, you're doing the visual equivalent of skipping the fundamentals because you're afraid of appearing to pander. A scientist told me, "Simpletons are those who do *not* start simple. If someone skips the basic presentation steps, I get suspicious." Therefore:

Present the Full Picture First

"The first thing I want to see is a histogram," said that same scientist. "Show me the distribution." When you argue in words, you should make your claim and then elaborate on it. The same is true when you add visuals: Argue from the whole to its parts, not the other way around. Failure to do this can make your reader suspicious that you're not arguing in good faith. Once you present the overview, you can move to its stronger and weaker component points.

Be Honest

Representation of anything necessarily involves assumptions. Be as honest about your assumptions as you can. If the data doesn't support what you want to say, then you should qualify, explain, or revise. Data can be wrong—and it's your job to check your data for accuracy. That's part of your responsibility as a writer. Maybe you know your data isn't precise, but you want to work with it anyway. (Political polls are an example of uncertain and imprecise data that analysts still want to study closely.) If your data is unclear, unstable, or otherwise not fully trustworthy, you should be up front about that fact.

Be Careful of the Details

Details matter because they build and enforce trust. If you're careless with the smaller stuff, you motivate the reader to distrust you on the bigger stuff. In data visualization, the small stuff can be complicated. Color perception is complex, for example. When one color blurs into another on a map, exact boundaries can be hard to discern. The proper use of color is difficult; how you choose and use it is very important.

Axes on a graph also matter. How you define them affects what the reader will see. The previous histogram depicting wealth

distribution shows how important these decisions are. What nu-
meric intervals will you use? (Plotting something from zero to
100 will look very different than plotting the same data from 90 to
100.) What are the boundaries of what your graph will measure?
And why are you choosing these particular boundaries?

This re-creation (based on an actual advertisement) makes
very basic mistakes:

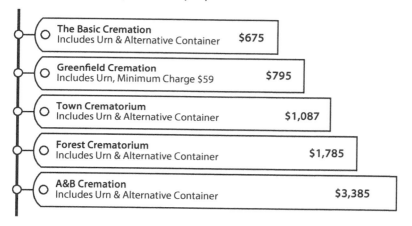

Cremation Service Cost Comparison
Price taken from phone survey September 2022

The Basic Cremation
Includes Urn & Alternative Container $675

Greenfield Cremation
Includes Urn, Minimum Charge $59 $795

Town Crematorium
Includes Urn & Alternative Container $1,087

Forest Crematorium
Includes Urn & Alternative Container $1,785

A&B Cremation
Includes Urn & Alternative Container $3,385

Each bar in this chart has its own unmentioned scale. That is,
there is no proportional relation between any of the bars. If there
were, the fifth entry (A&B Cremation) would be almost five times
the length of the first (The Basic Cremation). The Basic folks may
be honest cremators, but their advertising is visually misleading.

If you have a lot of data, there are many visual tricks you can
use to present it. *Try not to use any of them.* Instead, **anticipate
counterarguments and address them visually.**

Animation is another complicated technique that gives you
different ways to represent time and how data changes across
time. But you don't necessarily need it. Instead, you should aim
for the simplest, clearest presentation of your material. Here's
an example:

Case Study: The 2022 Kansas Abortion Referendum

The 2022 Kansas state referendum on amending the state constitution to ban abortion lost by 59 percent–41 percent, leaving the
constitution unamended. How best to represent the vote?

   This county-by-county visualization does a poor job of it:

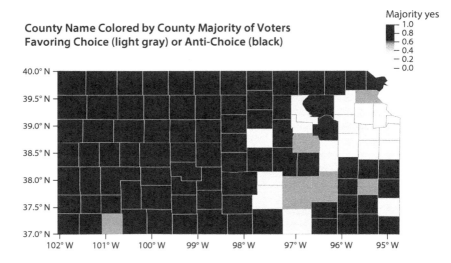

Here, the white shading indicates that a county voted for the
amendment, with black shading signifying a vote against, and gray
an even split. The map is obviously misleading. A reader with no
knowledge of the result might easily conclude that the anti-choice
side won—but it was decisively defeated. The diagram invites this
misunderstanding because it doesn't show that the most populous
counties voted for choice.

   The map also presents extraneous—and therefore distracting—
information, such as latitude and longitude. (A compass arrow pointing north would have served, and even that isn't really necessary.)

   We love maps, but we sometimes love them too well. When
all is said and drawn, a simple table of numbers may be the best
visual of all. Here's a list of votes by county (which I've abridged
to save space):

Table 1. Results by County

COUNTY	NO	YES	TOTAL VOTES	EST. RPT.
Johnson	69%	31%	248,904	>95
Sedgwick	58	42	142,691	>95
Shawnee	66	34	63,648	>95
Douglas	81	19	46,490	>95
Wyandotte	74	26	31,399	>95
Leavenworth	59	41	24,385	>95
Butler	50	50	21,590	>95
Reno	49	51	18,646	>95
Riley	68	32	16,963	>95
and so on, down to small counties:				
Clark	35	65	731	>95
Hodgeman	28	72	706	>95
Wichita	22	78	681	>95
Morton	32	68	637	95
Lane	40	60	607	95
Wallace	17	83	526	90
Hamilton	44	56	439	>95
Greeley	39	61	389	>95
Stanton	31	69	388	>95

Source: *Data from https://www.nytimes.com/interactive/2022/08/02/us /elections/results-kansas-abortion-amendment.html*

The list is less colorful and sexy than the diagram, but it's a lot clearer. Remember that *your goal is to communicate information, not wow the reader with cool graphic art.*

How to Test whether You're Doing Everything Right

I've offered many rules and suggestions in this chapter, all of them aimed at the goal of clear, crisp argument, from the blueprint (or outline) down to the nuts and bolts that hold the structure together. How you can tell whether you've done a good job at making an argument?

The afterlife of a piece of scholarly writing depends on how well (and easily!) it may be summarized.

Imagine you're recording a lecture about your work. Now imagine the audience listening to it. Here are two desirable takeaways:

1) The audience should listen with focus and ideally, pleasure; and
2) Members of the audience should be able to explain to someone else what you were talking about—and why they, too, should listen.

Without #1, you lose your listeners. Without #2, you don't get many new ones, so your work won't be sticky. In academic conversations, the main ingredient of stickiness is the ability to communicate compelling main ideas. Isn't that what a good story does?

In the end, a story works because the writer cares about telling it, and can communicate why others should care about it, too. This means caring enough to design the story properly.

CHAPTER 3

Jargon and Judgment

Most Difficulty Is Not Useful

Remember *Memento*? The movie, which came out in 2000, has an unusual premise: the main character is investigating a murder, but he has brain damage that prevents him from retaining new memories. He tries to keep track of the clues by tattooing his body with them. The movie's plot unspools out of order, in two consecutive sequences. The first one runs in reverse (from the end to the middle), and it's followed by another that runs forward from the beginning, where it meets the first sequence in the middle. *Memento* is, to put it mildly, hard to follow. The story disorients the viewer in some of the same ways that the main character is disoriented in the world—which is surely the point.*

Memento exemplifies what I'll call "useful difficulty." Useful difficulty produces challenging ambiguity that asks to be interpreted. It makes time-consuming demands. Perhaps that's why it so often appears in artwork, where interpretation creates meaning and is also part of the fun.

---

* The convolutions of *Memento* have proved catnip to many commentators. There's a Blu-Ray feature that allows you to watch the scenes in chronological order, but that's a different movie than the one that writer-director Christopher Nolan made. His film—and its meaning—can't be separated from the complications of his storytelling.

But rare is the occasion when those effects are appropriate in academic writing. And rare is the academic writer who can successfully execute them. In academic writing, ambiguous difficulty is mostly *not* useful, and it's almost never fun. As I've stressed throughout this book, academic writers usually can't afford to make those kinds of demands of their use-driven readers.

And yet they do. Why would a writer write in order to be understood only with difficulty? I would wager that only a few set out to be obscure. Instead, many academic writers fear being understood, so they make understanding elusive to protect themselves. I'm pretty sure that most of them don't do it on purpose, or realize that they're doing it. They're distracted by academic anxiety.

That anxiety comes from academia's professional culture. Younger writers risk something when they write. Students want a degree, and younger faculty members must publish or perish. It's understandable to feel anxious if your livelihood is at stake, hence the felt need to be seen as brilliant. Many academic writers (and not just young ones) fear that their ideas will be judged un-formidable, un-fascinating, un-*smart*.

Older writers keep the habit. Prestige and reputation continue to matter even after youth passes. Most scholars care about advancing their fields, but that's not the only reason they write. They also write to gain respect, and that's a nerve-wracking pursuit. Graduate students seek to be certified as experts. Certified experts (professors and others) put that credential on the line.

The culture of academic writing is shame-based. We fear being caught out, surrounded by colleagues clucking at our lack of preparation ("What? You missed that?"). But that's not even the worst fear. Worse is being exposed as a mediocre, a purveyor of pedestrian ideas. More than other writers, we fear being exposed as wanting. If we're not up to standard (or worse, wrong), we might be thought stupid.*

---

* Psychologists have identified a common anxiety dream in which the subject leaves the house without some (or all) of their clothes. The academic version typically

All writers have to figure out what their readers know and don't know. You don't need to define ionization for a chemist, or remind an American literature scholar that Moby Dick is colored white.

But as I suggested in chapter 1, academic anxiety invites the writer to go too far the other way. The scenario plays out this way. The writer imagines that experienced readers don't need things explained to them—and that such background will make those readers think they're being treated as clodpolls. The writer imagines the experienced reader saying, "You must think I'm a dunce—and that means you must be one yourself." From this imaginary interaction is born the fear of being branded stupid. It's a misplaced fear, and it has pernicious results. When academic writers (including a disproportionate number of dissertation writers) skip over the basics, the reader never gets comfortable.

The actual truth is that experts don't mind if you outline the fundamentals first. Ironically, that's how you communicate that you know your stuff, not by leaving things out that "everybody" already knows.

Here is the second sentence of a scholarly book:

When monastic reform was vigorously pursued under the influence of Benedict of Aniane at the councils of Aachen in 816 and 818/19, during the reign of Charlemagne's son and successor, Louis the Pius (814–40), it appeared that Carolingian reforms would endure.[1]

The author supplies the reader with no context or background here. If you're not already familiar with Benedict of Aniane, the councils of Aachen, and the Carolingian reforms, then the author is telling you "This book isn't for you." While we may safely assume

---

takes place in a classroom. The subject is clothed, but woefully unprepared for school. (In my common version of the dream, I have somehow missed weeks or months of class, and when I walk in, the final exam is about to be given.) For more about this dream, see Kelly Conaboy, "Why Adults Still Dream about School" (*The Atlantic*, September 22, 2022).

from her opening lines that the author doesn't expect to build a summer home with her book royalties, that doesn't mean that she should reduce her potential readership to a number that might fit into a school bus.

*So **don't assume that the reader already knows what you're talking about.*** Don't refer to "Hammett's Sam Spade short stories" without explanation. The reference is obscure and little-known outside of specialist niches. From this unexplained reference, a reader might infer that you don't deign to speak to a lightweight who doesn't know this apparent commonplace—and that brushoff would be felt by almost all scholars, to say nothing of general readers. Do you really want to alienate your readership like that?

Writing, Teaching

It's worth repeating that academic writers teach when we write. The "class" might be made up of specialists (think of a faculty seminar—or, for a writer, a niche journal for subspecialists). Or the audience might comprise experienced nonspecialists (an upper-level undergraduate or graduate seminar, or a journal that serves a whole field). Or they might be a group with less experience (a lower-level undergraduate class, or a meeting at the local public library—or, to follow the publishing analogy, a cross-disciplinary journal, or maybe a crossover magazine that reaches outside of academia). The audience may vary, but the teaching mission remains the same. You should want them to understand what you're saying.

Specialized audiences are rare—and besides, they probably know less than you think they do. Even if they know, remind them anyway. If you take too much background knowledge for granted, you disorient your reader from the start. Instead, you should lay out, step by step, points of background. Here's another passage from the opening to a book. Compare it to the one I just quoted:

In an age when every European explorer was racing to find new trade routes to Asia, Columbus approached several European monarchs to propose his westerly route. The king of Portugal said no. King Ferdinand and Queen Isabella of Spain twice rejected the proposal. Eventually, after his third attempt, they decided to let him try. The year was 1492. The Spanish monarchs had just waged the final, victorious campaign of Christian Reconquest, ending seven hundred years of Muslim control on the Iberian Peninsula.[2]

The author, Ada Ferrer, develops a more complex argument later, but as she sets out, we see her reminding her reader of the facts upon which it rests. Even though almost everyone knows that Columbus set sail in 1492, Ferrer is teaching, not pandering. You wouldn't start an undergraduate physics class by plunging into quantum theory because you were sure that everyone already understood Newtonian mechanics. The same goes for a writer: you should understand the needs of your audience and aim to include the largest swath of them that you can.

Furthermore

Yes, there is such a thing as too much background. If you intend to publish in a journal of analytic philosophy, you need not write as though a high-school student could read your work. But you would be well-served if a specialist in another branch of philosophy, or perhaps an intellectual historian, could follow along. I will have more to say about stretching the boundaries of your audience in chapter 4.

My point here is that even when writing to their fellow specialists, academic writers too often err on the side of providing too little background.

Which brings me to jargon and its discontents—and also its contents.

Jargon and Incivility

I've stressed that all writing is a story. Jargon is part of that story. It's easiest to explain what I mean by looking at a story. Consider the following sentences, the opening of chapter 22 of Charles Dickens's novel *Little Dorrit*:

> Mr Clennam did not increase in favour with the Father of the Marshalsea in the ratio of his increasing visits. His obtuseness on the great Testimonial question was not calculated to awaken admiration in the paternal breast, but had rather a tendency to give offence in that sensitive quarter, and to be regarded as a positive shortcoming of gentlemanly feeling.

Perhaps you find this passage difficult to understand. But if you're a member of the group who has read the earlier chapters, you know that it's funny. (It made me laugh when I read it.)

Here's an explanation: The narrator and the reader share a joke at the expense of old Mr. Dorrit, who is ironically called "the Father of the Marshalsea" because he's the longest-serving inmate at the debtors' prison of that name. Dorrit is dismayed that one of his regular visitors, Mr. Clennam, is not giving him money ("testimonials") each time he arrives. Dorrit assumes an air of gravity based on his seniority as a prisoner, and he looks down on Clennam as lacking good manners. Part of the joke is that Mr. Clennam is already acting secretly to aid Dorrit and his family. By assuming Dorrit's naïve and limited point of view, Dickens winks at the reader.

Readers of the first twenty-one chapters of the novel see this. As you read *Little Dorrit*—or any story—you become part of an in-group who knows the plot and characters. Because you know, you can get the jokes, which arise here from comic superiority to Mr. Dorrit. The narrator and the reader share a sly and confidential joke based on what they know and Mr. Dorrit doesn't.

Jargon operates the same way. Like the advancing plot of a story, *jargon enforces an in-group and an out-group*. The in-group knows what's going on, because they know what the terms mean, along with their implications. In the case of *Little Dorrit*, that knowledge opens the window to understanding the satiric irony in the passage I just quoted.

The in-group is a reading community. The out-group is excluded from it. When you use jargon, keep an eye on the membership of both groups.

Jargon doesn't have to involve big words. Inclusion and exclusion are what's important.* The history of chess offers a benign example. By the 1800s, a sufficient number of strong players begin to take the game seriously enough that schools of play began to develop. Today an experienced chess player knows what it means when you describe a player's style as "romantic" or "classical." A casual player probably won't. In a chess context, then, the words "romantic" and "classical" function as jargon.

Here are a few more malignant examples. (I'm numbering them because I'll return to them.):

(1) [S]tudents' production of texts and professor and peer response to those texts . . . provide an opportunity space for socialization into discursive practices, represent a central medium for the display of disciplinarity, and mediate the reproduction of disciplinary social structures as students achieve relative levels of "success" and "visibility." Situated examination of the way texts are produced and read

---

* Steve Martin has a great bit about a plumber telling a joke to another plumber (https://www.youtube.com/watch?v=-DvJHhAY9Qc). The gag illustrates the exclusionary nature of jargon. Neither the plumber's joke nor the punchline are accessible to non-plumbers (the out-group, which is also Martin's audience)—and that creates the joke.

within the activity structures of graduate programs is, thus, a key nexus for understanding disciplinarity.[3]

Tip
Scare quotes

Note the author's placement of quotation marks around the words "success" and "visibility" in #1 and "inauthentic" in #3. When you place scare quotes around a word, you raise a salient question: If you don't like this word, then why are you using it instead of a more accurate one?

Use quotation marks only for quotations. Instead of using scare quotes, find the best word instead. Mark Twain said that the difference between the right word and the "almost right word" is the difference between lightning and a lightning bug.

This passage comes to us from deep in the field of composition studies. A specialist in the field would probably understand it readily. Here's a paraphrase:

As graduate students write and receive feedback from professors and peers, this experience offers an opportunity to socialize the students into their discipline's discourse. Writing is a way that students display their familiarity with a discipline. They reproduce the discipline's norms and practices, especially as they achieve relative levels of success and visibility through their own writing. Disciplinarity, therefore, can be understood by examining graduate student writing, in the context of the programs and relationships where this writing is produced and assessed.[4]

I didn't write this paraphrase, but I like it much better than the published original. It breaks up an overlong sentence and eliminates clunky phrasing ("opportunity space") and unnecessary jargon ("disciplinary social structures"). Without sacrificing meaning, it welcomes more readers and makes things easier for the ones who can already figure it out.

But the next example can't easily be paraphrased:

> (2) [Serial killer Dennis] Nilsen dismembered bodies while blasting Aaron Copland's *Fanfare for the Common Man* on his personal stereo. (Conversely, Laurie Anderson's prosthetic ballad *O Superman* was another favorite.) As he expressed it: "I want crowds around me to listen to my solitude." The killer described the bonfire he made of the bodies he had taken apart as a return to a total natural unity: "A mixing of flesh in a common flame and a single unity of ashes . . . a uniform and anonymous corporation cemetery." He described his ultimate place in the mass public sphere as a sort of corporate and collective gathering point: or, more exactly, his final public service was as a mass spectacle of pathology and abjection. He was a black hole of violation and pollution about which the contemporary national body gathers, spectates, and discharges itself: in his words, he was "a national receptacle into which all the nation will urinate."[5]

The author focuses in this paragraph on a testament by a necrophiliac murderer, so we shouldn't expect the murderer's quoted passages about "unity" through cremation to make much sense. But the author's own explanation is scarcely easier to follow. What is "a black hole of violation and pollution about which the contemporary national body gathers"? The author uses one abstraction to explain another. He invents his own jargon as he goes along—and the reader has to struggle to enter his in-group of one.

This example gets cloudier as it goes along:

> (3) One must beware the figural status of national entities—those "imagined communities," in Benedict Anderson's

phrase. This is not to say that they are "inauthentic," or always irredeemably hypostatized; any community whose members are not immediately present to one another is necessarily constituted by some idea of itself, indeed by elaborate performative strategies of rhetorical self-constitution.[6]

This passage displays slippage ("national entities" are not the same thing as "imagined communities"). But the main problem lies in the author's reliance on abstractions ("inauthentic," "immediately present to one another," etc.) that receive no concrete illustrations to balance them. Such loose usage produces strange constructions. An imagined community may be hypostasized (which has various meanings), but by what moral yardstick may it be "irredeemably hypostatized"?

These excerpts come from published works by professors of reputation. Yet their careless use of jargon comes as no surprise. In his indispensable "Politics and the English Language," George Orwell provides examples of jargon from his own time to show how it bypasses clear thinking and thus inhibits clarity and understanding.* Jargon often does that. (I'll talk soon about when it doesn't.) In example #1 above, the author's use of phrases like "activity structures of graduate programs" to describe what happens in graduate seminars throws unnecessary, confusing obstacles in front of the reader.

As important is the fact that these passages are painful to read. The pain doesn't just come from riding over the bumps and shifts in the sentences. The pain comes from humiliation.

Bad academic writing inflicts a special form of humiliation. It's the feeling of shame that comes on when you just don't get some-

---

* Orwell's short essay, which he wrote in 1946, is widely available online. If you haven't read it, please do. I'll say more about Orwell's trenchant argument in the final chapter of this book.

thing that you think you're supposed to get. You read it, and you get lost. You push through it again, and maybe you get a few parts of it, and you try to bridge the gaps like an archaeologist inferring a full skeleton from a handful of bones. Sometimes you think you (maybe) get it (mostly) right. Sometimes you just can't make meaning out of it, so you push on to the next page and hope you haven't just skipped something crucial. Always you feel a sense of inadequacy.

Professors, including the writers of the above excerpts, are generally smart characters. But we often write in a way that makes communication harder—and in doing so, we set poor examples for those we teach (including our readers). Instead of yielding to inquiry, too much academic writing rebuffs it.

Why on earth would writers make their readers feel pain and shame? I suggested earlier that many authors—especially less experienced ones—write defensively out of anxiety. They fear being exposed and thought to be stupid. But the writers of these passages are established and well-respected, which makes the anxiety explanation less likely.

When writing is armed against readers, it erects barriers before them. To choose to communicate selectively—only with people with the intellect and determination to figure out (or try to figure out) what's being said in sentences of tortured and arthritic complexity—is elitist and separatist. Instead of being inclusive, it's also cruelly Darwinian: only the fittest readers survive.

Such writing invites the idea that it's most important to be cool: to be a member of an in-group within which prickly jargon takes the place of tattoos or matching leather jackets. The important thing is to create an "us" (who understand, or say they do) versus a "them" (who can't or won't).

Using jargon expressly to keep people out is a social act as well as a political one. To write that way is impolite, unfriendly, and just plain uncivil. To exclude readers purposefully and unnecessarily has potent implications. It's also just rude. Who wants to read a writer who's deliberately affronting you?

Furthermore
Case study: doctors

The history of medicine showcases a particularly obnoxious example of jargon that's intended to exclude. When doctors gained the professional authority we recognize today, during the decades surrounding the turn of twentieth century, the relation between doctors and patients became more hierarchical. As the social distance between doctors and patients increased, doctors deliberately used jargon (such as arcane Latin names for common nouns) to exclude patients from their conversations. In other words, doctors were advised to use jargon precisely to create their own in-group to prevent patients from understanding them. Ugh.

If you don't use your writing to help your reader understand, it will become an exercise rather than an outreach. Remember the clasp of the hand: writing is at heart a collegial, communal activity. It broadens circles—or ought to. It's friendly—or should be.

If jargon can help you be more friendly, then use it. But if it keeps readers out or toughens their task, then shun it.

In Search of Good and Civil Jargon
(Yes, It Is Out There)

What does good jargon look like? Most important, good jargon helps the reader because it's economical. Think of a computer macro. A "macro" (the word is itself an example of jargon) allows computer programmers to save time through shorthand. Let's say I've written a sequence of ten lines of code that allows me to search a database in a particular way that I do very often. I can then write a macro that will allow me to retrieve that entire chunk of code with just a couple of assigned keystrokes. I might type "sd"—the name of my macro for "search database"—and the ten lines will pop right up.

Now let's return from computer language to English. Imagine a phrase that is known and shared by an in-group that fully understands it. When lawyers talk to each other, they use phrases like "force majeure" and "stare decisis." These terms literally come from other languages, but between lawyers, they form their own language. Such phrases are like small icebergs: the visible words stand for a large cluster of ideas below the surface whose precise meaning is shared. When lawyers talk to each other, their jargon allows them to invoke these clusters quickly through the use of compact terminology. That's an example of good and friendly jargon. It enables efficient communication.

Most groups of professionals—including academics in their individual disciplines—have their own jargon for this purpose. Stockbrokers speak to each other about "puts" and "calls," while coin collectors discuss different "mint states." The word "panel" will have different meanings among groups of conference organizers, interior decorators, artists, architects, woodworkers, and hairdressers. But in each case, people understand each other—as long as they all belong to the same in-group.

Jargon depends on audience. To use it successfully, you have to know who you're talking to. If you use professional jargon when you address a mixed audience, you'll invite some readers in and push others out. If you're not sure who's in your audience, explain your technical terms, or don't use them at all.

Jargon also requires precision. When one accountant talks to another about asset classes, they'll understand each other because the term has a precise meaning. But one of the many risks that accompany the use of jargon is that a term of art may lose that precise meaning.

For example: the verb "to map" started with certain popular meanings having to do with actual geographical plots. Then the word was taken up by theorists of discourse and territorial organization, who used it as jargon in precise ways. No problem so far.

But—and this is a common shift—the word underwent "semantic generalization," meaning that it became a catch-phrase for different clusters of ideas. Now it's used willy-nilly without reference to its specific meaning. For example:

> [A]n automated system called the Allegheny Family Screening Tool was used to determine which families were in need of child welfare assistance . . . [G]iven the large amount of data the system processed (and the sensitivity of the data), it carried a serious risk of data breaches. Each of these prior concerns . . . maps onto concerns regarding equality, and privacy.[7]

The last sentence of the passage invites misreading due to a lack of precision and concreteness. If the author wants to describe how an automated system carries risks that invoke existing concerns about privacy, it would be simpler and clearer to just say that.

As this example suggests, semantic generalization can produce bad writing: it's hard to visualize the "mapping" the writer describes. Mapping is only part of the problem here, but that shouldn't be surprising, as indiscriminate use of jargon travels easily with other problems of clarity and intelligibility. *If a term has lost its clarity and you still want to use it, redefine it for your own purposes to make it useful again.*

An instructive example of this loss of clarity, from my own discipline of literature, is the use of the word "text."

The Unpleasures of the "Text"

This story is for everyone, not just the literary critics who love the word. There's a larger message to the tale, namely that **all jargon**

carries a risk of imprecision. Jargon isn't necessarily imprecise, but it can become so—as "text" did. The message to all writers is that *the abstractness of jargon requires constant vigilance on the part of the user.* The uses and misuses of "text" show the need to handle jargon with care.

The problem arises because the word "text" has become an example of social signaling. If you listen to a group of professional literature scholars talk to each other, you'll hear talk about texts. A professor giving a talk about Frederick Douglass's first autobiography might talk about "Douglass's text." A scholar of satiric poetry might say that "the text" is written in heroic couplets. Dropping the word "text" into conversation (oral or written) in this way shows how the use of academic jargon marks someone as a member of a particular social group.

When students join these conversations, they quickly pick up the lingo. As they socialize themselves into this professional world, they try to sound like their elders. Saying "text" instead of story (or "visual text" instead of film) makes you sound like you belong in the club. So the habit reproduces itself.

The word "text" substitutes for a variety of more precise descriptors. I've seen many experienced scholars use "text" instead of a term that tells the audience exactly what kind of literary work—a novel, a poem—they mean. The results can be needlessly confusing. In the following short excerpt, the writer presents a compelling insight about a seventeenth-century Mexican poet's use of Latin. But overreliance on the word "text" makes the passage hard to follow:

> Her text inscribes itself in the margins of the conventional text, supplementing it. The mask of the male voice dissembles the possible meaning of the text.[8]

This passage exemplifies how a word can be repeated so often that it loses its meaning.

TEXT BOX

"Text" actually has several clear definitions, including the most recent one connected to cell phones. People who specialize in textual criticism use the word "text" in careful and precise ways. They might talk about "textual variants" of a poem (in a case where the poet might have left multiple handwritten versions, say). Here's a sentence from an article discussing Langston Hughes's translation of Federico García Lorca's "Blood Wedding":

> Of the three versions of the same text, it is Hughes's version that seems most poetic, active, and vital.

"Text" may be used to refer to the actual words in a printed source (as opposed to the pictures—if you're talking about comic books, say—or what book historians call "paratext," which can include not only pictures but also the cover of a book, advertisements that appear alongside an article in a magazine, and so on). You might say, for example, that "The back cover of *Fly Me to the Moon* suggests a romance, but the text tells another story, about space travel."

Or you could refer to "the text" as distinct from the footnotes, as I did when I was talking about citation in chapter 2.

Or you might speak of a novel that was bowdlerized and then restored (such as Richard Wright's *Native Son*) as having a 1940 text and a 1995 text. But you should not say, "Bigger Thomas is the protagonist of Wright's text." In the latter case, you should say "Wright's novel"—unless, of course, you're a deconstructionist.

The word "text" has a scriptural meaning as well, as in this passage:

> It is your own personal encounter with this text that I want to encourage, and by struggling directly with Marx's text, you can begin to shape your own understanding of his thought.

What's the reason for this blurry usage? The recent history of "text" explains how the term that has lost its onetime stability and become socially marked jargon. It's a just-so story of poststructuralism.

When the interpretive strategy of "deconstruction" emerged in literary studies in the 1960s, its proponents argued that literature lacks the coherence that previous critics had attributed to it. Language, they said, is unstable and always incomplete—and so is anything that's made out of language. And so, therefore, is meaning itself.

As a result, deconstructionists deeply distrusted the idea of literary form. These critics and theorists saw such formal categories as novel, essay, or poem as untrustworthy, unreliable labels. Instead, they argued that writing should be examined at the level of language, with the goal of uncovering the contradictions, incoherence, and instability of meaning that lay there.

Furthermore

The word "deconstruction" has, in past decades, gradually separated itself from the technical practice of deconstructive criticism and taken on a life of its own. In common usage, the word "deconstruct" now means simply "take apart" or "disassemble." You can now deconstruct a car or eat a "deconstructed egg roll."

This is another case of unstable jargon: the meaning of the original word becomes imprecise in a way that would presumably delight a literary deconstructionist.

So deconstructionists didn't talk about novels or poems. They pointedly refused those labels. Instead, they talked about "texts" in order to flag their refusal. Because literary forms don't provide reliable or meaningful distinctions, they contended, those distinctions had to collapse. Writing of any kind could only be a text.*

The proliferation of "text" in today's scholarship is an unrecognized legacy of deconstruction. It's a habit that hung around after the party ended. Most literary scholars today believe that form means something. Presented with essays and poems about war, for instance, they'll mark differences based on form. But many of them still reflexively describe these works as "texts," like this:

> Syntactic peculiarities of the Rg Vedic language have been widely used to create the special, suggestive style of the text.[9]

Here the use of "text" simply substitutes a vague word for a precise one.

The heyday of deconstruction and other poststructuralist literary theories lasted a generation or so. It petered out in the 1990s and, like all interpretive strategies, gave way to other ways of reading and thinking. But deconstruction left an ironic precipitate. The habit of using the word "text" has persisted, but without reference to deconstruction. When today's scholars study literary form, they continue to use a word whose modern usage was devised to undermine the whole idea of literary form!

"Text" has thus become an anachronism that is used without any consciousness of how history has made it into one. Once upon a time, deconstructionists used to seize upon just that sort of contradiction.

"Text" is a glaring example of jargon that has lost its specificity, and its point. The continued casual use of the word demonstrates how intellectuals can be socialized into a field of study without

---

* Adding to the complications, in the postmodern world, *anything* can be a text, not just writing. This malleability makes it possible to "inscribe the Chinese woman's body in political structures," as in an example in the last section of this chapter.

being taught its recent history. So they use a word without realizing what it means, and it makes everyone involved look bad.

Use the word "text" by all means. But if you do, use it precisely.

The Abstract and the Concrete

A special danger accompanies uncareful use of jargon: a lack of clarity and vividness and an overreliance on abstraction. Because jargon is a form of shorthand, it compresses information: a good example is the alphabet stew of acronyms and initialisms that characterizes military communication. Good jargon is specific, but it's almost never vivid. ***When you use jargon, you have to be sure to supply concrete detail to support it***, because the abstract requires the concrete for balance and support. (This lack of balance is one of the main problems with example #3 that I quoted earlier in this chapter.)

There's a general principle lurking here:

Academic arguments—and all other arguments—depend on the alternation of the abstract and the concrete to make persuasive sense. The abstract organizes thought, while the concrete exemplifies it.

Academic writers are most prone to excesses of abstraction because they fail to think along with the reader and anticipate her questions. The only way to make a thesis clear is to throw a lasso around it and pull it down to earth. This discussion of court cases demonstrates the difficulties that result when the argument stays in the sky, too far away to see clearly:

These divergent interpretations of Filipino eligibility for U.S. citizenship can be understood as manifesting the contradictions embedded in the construct "American national." A compromise category, one created to resolve the rupture to American exceptionalism that U.S. occupation of the Philippines represented, it did not address so much as cover over under-lying incongruities narrated as the "Philippine problem." The inconsistencies across these adjudications of U.S. citizenship eligibility manifest the irresolution of that "problem." U.S. ambivalence over its occupation of the Philippines, together with its attempts to regulate the racialized identity of Amer-ica, conditions the uncertainty of the Filipino case in the eyes of the law. That is, that the courts could make such contrary decisions evidences how Filipino subjectivity has been consti-tutively constructed to resist sustainable visibility within the representational grids of the U.S. nation.[10]

The proliferation of abstract subjects ("rupture to American ex-ceptionalism," "representational grids of the U.S. Nation," and so on) means that the writer is relying on the reader to figure out what these things mean. That may be possible, but it greatly increases the effort that it takes to read the passage.*

The concrete doesn't just make the abstract intelligible. It also brings necessary persuasive force to the argument. Instead of gen-eral remarks about how large rain forests are and how rapidly they're being destroyed, the reader needs specifics. For example: "In 2016, a record of 29.7 million hectares of forest disappeared. That's 290,000 square kilometers, or an area almost the size of Italy or the state of Nevada." The smoke from that year's for-est fires was visible from outer space.[11] Without the concrete details—which create the compelling comparisons—the claim is unmemorable, and therefore unpersuasive.

The abstract and the concrete form a binary star, each orbiting about the other, bound together by gravity. In writing, the two need each other. Without the concrete, abstract concepts fly into the ether, where the reader can only squint at them and

---

* Notice, too, how Latinate constructions convey the abstractions here. Simple, direct exposition usually avoids these twisty words. ***Don't be afraid to write simply.***

conjecture about their meaning. But without the abstract to provide a blueprint, the concrete is just a pile of bricks.

The necessary link between the abstract and the concrete is easiest to see in experimental science. Scientists conduct experiments to test a theory (which is abstract). The results of their experiments (the concrete) will provide evidence to support or contradict that theory. Without the evidence, the theory remains an untested idea. Without the theory, the results are just numbers. *Any writer who makes an argument—and that includes all academic writers—must bring the abstract and the concrete together.*

Here's an example of how *not* to do this:

> I will show how the university is conducive to the exchange of ideas about what ought to be done in society, and because of this, clearer understandings and greater agreement on commonly-held truths result.

Abstractions here are supported by other abstractions, and the result is a squishy thesis statement that doesn't answer questions so much as raise them: Conducive how? What ideas? What ought to be done in society? Understandings of what? What kinds of commonly held truths? The law of relativity? Red skies at night, sailor's delight?

And another bad example:

> Redesigning the welfare state can be the engine of a long overdue change to social dynamics.

First, this statement introduces a metaphor that the reader can't visualize. The writer compares a redesign to an engine. What would that look like? Second—and relatedly—the statement is blurry. What are "social dynamics" anyway, especially in relation to the welfare state? Finally, the writer is force-feeding the reader a set of assumptions. Who says that social dynamics have to be changed? And why? Maybe the rest of the essay will explain, but that seems unlikely.

As you can see from these examples, the decoupling of the abstract and the concrete produces not only dense and difficult writing but also careless thinking. To think your sharpest thoughts, maintain the link between the abstract and the concrete. Here is a paragraph written by Adam Gopnik that beautifully balances them. My annotations are in the margins.

Romanticism under stress always becomes expressionism—what happened to Poe is also what happened to Fitzgerald. When a lyric writer cracks, there's a new kind of dissonant music in the breaking. The best passages in Fitzgerald's novels always worked better as fable and fairy tale than as realistic fiction. The most fantastical of his stories, "The Diamond as Big as the Ritz" and "The Curious Case of Benjamin Button," haunt us more than the neatly journalistic, mirror-of-their-time stories, like "May Day" and "The Rich Boy." Fitzgerald himself knew that the real weakness of his best novel was that we could not imagine Gatsby and Daisy reunited—that, in plain English, he could not evoke them rutting because he could not credibly imagine it.[12]

Gopnik starts with the argument that structures this paragraph. It takes the form of an abstraction—which means that it must be explained before long.

Here, Gopnik elaborates on his argument, stating it in a different way.

In this sentence, Gopnik suggests that Fitzgerald is a romantic, and so makes Fitzgerald's fiction an example of what Gopnik is talking about in his opening sentence.

Concrete evidence to support the preceding statement that Fitzgerald is a romantic and not a realist.

Here is the concrete illustration of the abstraction, an example drawn from Fitzgerald's most famous novel, The Great Gatsby. *The idea of the two lovers coming together is an impossibility, Gopnik says, which "stresses" the story and causes the characters to turn into ideas rather than possible people.*

Look how Gopnik goes back and forth between generalized abstractions (about unstable "romanticism") that he attributes to Fitzgerald, and concrete evidence from his stories (the insubstantial, ethereal quality of Gatsby and Daisy in *The Great Gatsby*) that explains what he means. This pendulum movement allows the reader to follow theory into example and then back again.

You may introduce a thought with an idea or an example—that is, start a thought with the abstract or the concrete. But whichever one you begin with will soon have to give way to the other, or else the reader will get lost—or wonder whether you are. *The reader needs to see the concept illustrated (abstract → concrete), or else the example invoke the concept (concrete → abstract).*

New Pictures Tell Stories. Old Ones Don't.

Pictures are the opposite of abstractions. I wrote in chapter 1 of how the vividness of metaphors brings pictures to mind. That vividness helps writers teach their work. In chapter 2 I described how arguments—and paragraphs—are stories, meaning that they have a narrative logic that allows readers to follow along.

Metaphors make pictures that illustrate a writer's stories. As I explained in chapter 1, part of their power arises from their distinctiveness and the economy that results from the collapse of unlike terms into a single phrase. "Glass ceiling" is an example of a metaphor that illustrates its meaning so powerfully that it remains effective more than forty years after the phrase was coined.[13]

But if a metaphor is overused, it loses the ability to invoke an image. To "coin a phrase," the idiom I just used in the last paragraph, once invoked a picture of a press that mints shiny coins, but now most people just use it to refer to a clever verbal invention. You probably read right past it just now. If I mentioned "the body of an essay," you'd probably blast right past that too. And when we "cc" an email, we're using an abbreviation for "carbon copy" when no actual paper is involved. Orwell calls these phrases "dead metaphors." Many dead metaphors turn into jargon—and there's nothing necessarily wrong with using them if everyone agrees on their meaning.*

But if jargon obscures meaning, then trouble ensues. "Activity structures of graduate programs" (from #1 above) isn't clearer than "graduate classrooms" and makes the reader do more work to figure it out. Worse, a "class-based axis of oppression" can invoke either a nonexistent graph (what is the other axis?) or else a nonexistent military alliance, and so weakens the author's indictment of oppression on the basis of class. Some examples from the early 2020s might include "quiet quitting" and "acting your wage," which depoliticize and infantilize the actions that they describe. "Enhanced interrogation techniques" is a nefarious example of jargon that blunts affect and discourages readers from reacting to a subject (torture) that they may care very much about. Inversely, we have in recent years witnessed a shift from "global warming" to "climate change" to "climate crisis," as scientists have struggled to come up with a term that communicates the seriousness and urgency of the issue.

Or jargon can fall in between creating meaning and obscuring it. The term "neoliberalism" has become jargon in a number of humanities and social science fields, but its meaning isn't precise—it swings around conceptual poles instead of being semantically tethered. People from different disciplines will acquire various understandings of neoliberalism. The word variously conveys implications of capitalism, privatization, globalization, stratification, inequality, and competition, among other ideas. Because neoliberalism is a broad word, its meaning doesn't arrive at once. Rather, it accretes: you get a sense of it over time, in relation to your own disciplinary context, and that sense can remain hazy.

When you, the writer, enter conceptual haze, you risk losing hold of your reader's hand. So you need to be especially careful.

---

* A few other examples that come quickly to mind: "break the ice" (which originated with ice-breaking ships), "stuffed shirt" (which probably refers to a scarecrow), and "neck and neck" (which once referred only to horse racing).

Using "neoliberalism" as jargon carries risk because you can't be assured of agreement about what the word means. It's an example of a shortcut you should take with care (know your audience!), not only because the chance for imprecision is high but especially because the word is emotionally loaded.

If you start throwing around a blurry term as jargon (that is, believing that everyone understands it the same way you do), you create ambiguity. You also annoy your reader—and that's bad for the relationship. The solution: **When you rely on a hazy word, define it for your own purposes when you first use it.** Here's how to do it:

> I define neoliberalism as a political and economic philosophy whose proponents espouse free markets and privatization of state enterprises as the mode by which prosperity and democracy are best reached. These policies, which include IMF interventions, NAFTA, shifts in immigration policy, the escalation of border industrialization initiatives, and varied austerity programs have also created the conditions for many of the most tumultuous events in the Americas in the last forty years.[14]

Clearly wary of the volatility of the word "neoliberalism," the writer, Patricia A. Ybarra, explains in exemplary fashion what she means by it, so that there will be no misunderstanding between her and her readers.

You can generalize this solution, because **you can make your own jargon**. And when you need it, you should. **Or you can borrow it from your sources, characters, or interviewees.** Elevate their pithiest phrases into jargon that you can then use as an analytical and expressive tool. At the beginning of this chapter I invented the term "useful difficulty" and explained what I meant by it. Now I can use it freely in this book, because you (my reader) and I belong to an in-group that understands the term. But if you don't explain the phrases you invent (as the writer does not in example #2 above), then you'll make things worse for your reader, not better.

Judgment Calls

How can you tell when jargon is being helpful or unhelpful? Like most writing choices, this is a judgment call. Approach the judgment with an eye to community-building with your reader. I said earlier that jargon creates an in-group (which understands it) and an out-group (which doesn't). The in-group is a reading community, and the out-group stands outside it. When you use jargon, ask yourself:

- Are you helping the in-group?
- Are you excluding anyone you would like to include in it?

These questions will help to preserve a good relationship with your reader.

If you use jargon in your writing, look over your draft and ask yourself whether it is of the good or bad variety:

- *Good jargon should be descriptive* and point to what is being summarized or encapsulated. "The frontier theory of history," a term introduced in 1893 that still possesses a clear meaning, is a case in point.
- *Good jargon should be efficient.* It should make reading easier for members of the reading community: The terms "hypotaxis" and "parataxis," for example, don't have obvious meanings, but they communicate precisely within their in-group. They refer to sentence structure. "Hypotactic" describes sentences with dependent clauses, like this one:

  A style handbook that includes all kinds of writing rules looks suspicious, and that's because the writer inserts his own ego—surely an inflated one—into the middle of everything.

A paratactic sentence may have multiple clauses, but they aren't subordinated:

I opened this style handbook, and the author immediately assaulted me with rules.

- *Good jargon should not be used to keep people out. Instead, it builds a bridge between those in the know and those who aren't.* The phrase "free-range kids," invented by parenting expert Lenore Skenazy, is a good example, because you can get halfway to its meaning on sight. (Its thematic opposite, "helicopter parenting," has the same virtues.)

Furthermore

Lionel Trilling says his teacher Elliott Cohen taught him "that no idea was so difficult and complex but that it could be expressed in a way that would make it understood by anyone to whom it might conceivably be of interest."

I'm not sure this statement is always true, but it's a worthy sentiment and a good aspiration for academic writers to keep in mind.

- *Bad jargon includes terms that were never precisely defined, or whose definition is being debated.* Use these terms at your own risk—and if you do, define them as you introduce them. "Foucauldian worldview" falls into this category. The term lacks precision because the theorist Michel Foucault wrote on many subjects. For example, in the following sentence, the author is trying to define the key term, but the attempt collapses due to self-referential abstraction:

> In the Foucauldian worldview, relations of power and knowledge are articulated through discourse, which is both a language and a practice that brings into existence an object of knowledge.[15]

- *Bad jargon is politicized* (and therefore, what should the author do?). "Trickle-down economics" has a clear-enough meaning, but the term carries enormous political freight, which can easily distract the reader.
- *Bad jargon has undergone semantic generalization and no longer activates any precise scholarly meaning.* A good example from this category is "market disruption," which has escaped its original professional context to become an everywhere-applied cliché that now, in its current blurry state, does no more than gesture toward the general idea of disturbance.
- *Bad jargon is a term that belongs to many different fields and is defined differently in each.* For example, "liberalism."

The moral of this story is not to avoid jargon always. Nor is it to always welcome jargon with open arms. Make your judgments deliberately. Know when you're making them. And maintain this caution: **Jargon is an intoxicant, so limit your use of it**. One dose can lead to another, and the buildup can impair judgment. Overindulgence can produce prose that reads like an obstacle course, like this:

Reading the writing, publication, and adaptation history of *Native Son* tracks the overlap between journalism, sensationalism, fiction, and film as representations of crime provide the way to work through human behavior and morality as well as the underlying tensions and inadequacies of democratic order itself. In particular, such a reading shows how state and cultural institutions intersect with the political and economic systems allied within twentieth-century American democracy and the meanings created at this intersection through crime lead the citizenry to conceive of threats to order through individual crimes and imagine protection from these threats through expanded punitive apparatuses.

This paragraph is muddy. The technocratic language is hard to read and decipher. The problems don't arise from jargon alone: the sentences are overlong, tangled, and unnecessarily complex, so the reader has to pick them apart. But those tangles result in part from an uncritical embrace of jargon, by which I mean a willingness to rely on terms that convey big clumps of meaning ("state and cultural institutions," "democratic order," and so on) that the author hasn't defined for the purpose at hand.

Such usage lowers the reader into the swamp that William Strunk warned against. The author is saying (I think) that the reception of different versions of Richard Wright's *Native Son* in various media within a stratified and unequal democracy shows how crime stories persuade people that their lives and livelihoods are being threatened, and that they should turn to the police and the courts ("law and order") for protection. So why not just say that? Remember that **careless use of jargon usually invites other forms of imprecision** and a general loss of control over your material.

As you make your judgment calls, then, remember that jargon can alter consciousness. If it makes you drunk, you will drive your train of thought—with your reader as passenger—into a ditch. *Handle jargon with care—and always with concern for your reader.*

Some Common Mistakes and What They Show Us

Following is a very incomplete listing of various usage errors. I haven't tried to be systematic—and I've avoided some that really bug me—but instead have focused on words and phrases that point to larger lapses in precision, or a failure to consider the needs of the reader. Some of these common mistakes connect to problems that I've already identified. For example, passive voice (which obscures responsibility for action) naturally goes with waffling placeholders that defer the up-front statement of an argument. A few of these examples are jargon, but most are not. However, all of these errors commonly occur in the presence of jargon, because careless use of jargon is usually accompanied by lack of care elsewhere. *

Be Direct, Be Responsible

Avoid the passive voice. The passive results when the object of an action becomes the subject of a sentence describing that action, as in: "The ball was thrown against the wall." As is usually the case with passive voice, the subject disappears (who threw the ball?).

This tendency to efface the subject conceals responsibility for action: it avoids the question of who did it. As it does here:

> Sailors' boardinghouses, specifically, accommodated a population of the city that was marginalized not only by the nature of the sailors' work, but also by their foreignness, the diverse native cultures that they brought ashore with them, and their isolation from the conventions of respectable society.[16]

One may well ask who is doing the marginalizing here. This sort of deflection of responsibility characterizes the passive voice. The most famous example of weasel-like passive evasiveness is the non-admission admission by President Ronald Reagan in 1987 that "mistakes were made" during the Iran-Contra scandal.[17] (Made by whom? And on whose watch?) For this and other reasons, bureaucrats often prefer the passive voice.

But writers should not. If you've got something to say, say it and own it.†

---

* Please write to me if you have other good examples to share.

† An exception: when scientists describe an experiment, the action usually takes precedence over the actor, so it becomes acceptable to say "A solution of hydrochloric acid was added." For more on this subject, see https://gwc.ucr.edu/sites/default/files/2019-01/Scientific-Writing-Active-and-Passive-Voice.pdf.

On Big Words

The logophilic language expert Laurence Urdang had fun with words. In his introduction to *The New York Times Everyday Reader's Dictionary of Misunderstood, Misused, Mispronounced Words* (1972) he described his book this way:

> Not a succedaneum for satisfying the nympholepsy of nulli-fidians, it is hoped that the haecceity of this enchiridion of arcane and recondite sesquipedalian items will appeal to the oniomania of an eximious Gemeinschaft whose legerity and sophrosyne, whose Sprachgefühl and orexis will find more than fugacious fulfillment among its felicific pages.[18]

This kind of display is good fun, but it also points to a serious truth: ***Keep it simple***. As one writer says, "No one will be convinced if you use twenty-dollar words to express a ten-cent thought."[19]

Build off

Imagine building on something. O.K., now stop. I expect there's a picture in your head.

Now imagine building *off* the same structure. It's not the same thing. The details matter.

Concerted

By definition, a "concerted effort" is an action that involves more than one person. It takes multiple people—at least two—to act in concert.

This example, and the previous one, demonstrate the need to ***think purposefully about the words you use so you can choose the right ones***.

Conversely

"Conversely" is one of the most misused expressions in written English—which is perhaps another way of saying that its usage is changing. But if it's going to change, let's at least review what it still means.

Converse is a mathematical relation: If $Y \rightarrow Z$ (that is, if Y leads to Z), then the converse is $Z \rightarrow Y$. It works the same way with verbal statements. If I say, "When you open your mouth, I throw an M&M at it," then the converse of that statement would be: "When I throw an M&M at your mouth, you open it."

Along with a converse, every statement also has an *inverse*: **Not Y → Not Z**. Or, in words: "When you *don't* open your mouth, I *don't* throw an M&M at it."

And finally, every statement also has a *contrapositive*: **Not Z → Not Y**, or: "When I *don't* throw an M&M at your mouth, you *don't* open it."

In writerly practice, the converse is widely and often mistaken for the inverse. The writer of example #2 above misuses "conversely." So does even as bright a luminary as the anthropologist Mary Douglas:

> The more material that an elaborate technology imposes between ourselves and the satisfaction of our infantile desires, the more busily has sublimation been at work. But the converse seems questionable. Can we argue that the less the material basis of civilization is developed, the less sublimation has been at work?[20]

Let's look more closely at this passage by shearing away the verbiage surrounding the core assertions. Douglas starts by suggesting that technology causes "sublimation" ($Y \rightarrow Z$). Then she asks if less technology leads to less sublimation (Not Y → Not Z). But that's not the converse of the original statement; it's the inverse.

Common usage may eventually allow "converse" to stand for any sort of reversal. (This would be an example of the "semantic generalization" that I described earlier.) I hope that doesn't happen. If it does, the language will lose some valuable specificity. Right now, though, confusing converse and inverse is a mistake. If you care about good academic writing, I hope you'll make good judgment calls here. And the converse is also true: If you make good judgment calls . . .

The False "if"

Avoid writing sentences with a false "if/then" conditional clause. For example:

> If *The Sopranos* repeatedly risks a hard-won audience identification with Tony Soprano, then Bret Easton Ellis's *American Psycho* shows what happens when an author tries to operate without one.[21]

The author (who is, um, me) fails to create a condition (in which one thing depends on another). If you subtract the "if" and "then" from this sentence, its meaning is unchanged—and its economy is improved. Here's another example:

> If Elvis Presley invokes the agony of suspicion in "Suspicious Minds," Elvis Costello offers a full anatomy of the emotion in "Suspect My Tears."

The "if" in each of these cases isn't really an "if" anything. Instead, both are full-fledged propositions, assertions that don't depend on any conditions. *Avoid the false conditional.*

Impactful

Once upon a time, not all that long ago, you could only impact a tooth. Well, you couldn't, exactly. Impact wasn't a verb, but it did allow an adjective. A tooth can, as any dentist will tell you, become "impacted."

But ideas and people weren't the same as teeth, at least not until recently. Today, anything and anyone can be impacted—"positively" or "negatively." For example, a team of medical school teachers discovered that "both preparing to teach and teaching positively impact learning outcomes for peer teachers."[22] I think they're saying that doing your homework and then practicing your teaching will make you a better teacher.

Usage, the ultimate arbiter, is gradually making "impact" into a verb. I believe I can accommodate to that change, if it comes to that. (All right, I suppose it has.) But please, let us draw the line at positive and negative impacts. And users of the word "impactful" deserve a negative impact upside the head.

Importantly

Break the habit, if you've acquired it, of beginning a sentence with a word such as "Importantly" or "Tellingly" or "Fascinatingly." As every good creative writing teacher says: "Show, don't tell." In other words, make your assertion important, telling, or fascinating, and don't instruct your reader to find it so. You have no right—or ability!—to compel feeling on the part of your reader or anyone else. You have to earn that response with your writing.

Incredible

Whenever you use any form of the word "incredible," pause to consider its literal meaning (literally, not believable). Most of the time, you will choose another word.

The problem here comes from common usage. "Incredible" is overused in speech, and that keeps it nearer at hand than it should be. (The same goes for its synonym "unbelievable" and their cousin "amazing.") *Be cautious about writing with adjectives that you hear a lot.*

Inscribe

The frequency with which writers "inscribe" (or "reinscribe") ideas suggests that we're all walking around with styluses (ahem, styli) rather than pens.

Words like "inscribe" (and also "map," which I mentioned earlier) exemplify the problems posed by semantic generalization, the process by which they acquired multiple meanings and myriad uses. For example:

> Inscribed by multiple-layered, intersecting geopolitical powers at play, the Chinese woman's body in this narrative functions

For Example
A case study in semantic generalization

"Problematic" exemplifies how jargon may undergo multiple semantic shifts.

First, this common word becomes jargon by undergoing semantic specialization. In this case, "problematic" was specialized as a noun in the philosophy of Louis Althusser and Michel Foucault. They understood a text's "problematic" as its ideological background.

This move led to the word's popularization among academics. (It's constantly used by scholars in the humanities.) But due to readers' tendencies toward imprecision, the term then underwent generalization, and it fell back to its previous, less specific meaning. Now, it just means anything that seems to be some kind of problem.

And then there is a third shift: euphemization. Often, people say "This is problematic" when what they're shying away from is something worse (like "This is illegal"). In that event, "problematic" becomes an easy out for a writer who doesn't want to speak frankly.

as a site where the conflicts among these forces are staged and subversion against them emerged.[23]

As you can see, semantic generalization can produce impenetrable academese. This sentence is hard to understand because the author is assuming that the reader will be able to interpret all of the code words, not just "inscribe."

Sociolinguistically speaking, semantic generalization just happens sometimes. (It happened to "neoliberalism," and that's part of the reason why that word is hard to use as jargon.) The solution cannot be to leave inscription entirely to tattooists and other artisans—but neither can it be to accede to the use of "inscribe" to describe almost any form of lasting influence. So what to do? The answer, as it so often must be, is to stay aware and make good judgment calls. And *avoid using words that have lost semantic precision, unless you define them precisely for your own purposes.*

Interrogate

Do not "interrogate a text" unless you plan to waterboard it in the event that it equivocates.

I heard a joke in the same vein some years ago, about a fellow literary critic who said to an Irish literature specialist that the IRA cease-fire wouldn't affect his work because all his theories had already been exploded.

Overuse of words such as "interrogate" and "explode" dulls their real meaning and turns them into weary, abstract clichés. For words to have force, you need to use them precisely and concretely, and not use them too much. *Avoid tired phrases*, because when they become worn out, it's easy to forget what they actually mean. At best, tired phrases result in boring prose. At worst—well, you see from these examples that embarrassing prose may result.

So if you plan to "intervene" in a critical debate, wear a rain-coat. Or if you're prudent, body armor.

It is . . . that

It is the wordiness of the "It is . . . that" construction that makes your sentences, paragraphs, and essays run too long.

The solution is surprisingly clean amputation: simply cut out those three words and watch your sentences glide forward, unburdened of their extra mass. (Try doing that with the sentence that I wrote to introduce this idea just now.) Another example:

> ~~It is t~~The transitional quality of crepuscular light ~~that~~ makes it attractive to painters.

(For the sequel to this rewritten sentence, look at "Use Verbs" below.)

The *-ize* suffix

Adding *-ize* to a word vulgarizes a writer's efforts. It pulverizes delicacy, and with it writerly grace. So avoid:

Diagonalize
Ideologize
Instrumentalize
Neoliberalize
Operationalize
Problematize
Regularize
Virtualize
Weaponize

and most other *-ize* words that needlessly jargonize your writing.

Proactive

"Proactive" means "active in advance" (perhaps to head off a possible outcome), but it's usually used as a needless (and incorrect) synonym for "active." Be active in avoiding words that muddy the living language.

Societal

Human beings are social animals, so they should avoid the word "societal." "Social" refers to human relations in general and particular, while "societal" refers only to the entire social system. So in most cases, "social" will be the right word.

"Societal" is jargon, a term from sociology that escaped its disciplinary moorings and floated into the linguistic mainstream. Let us perform our social duty and return it to the discipline where it belongs.

The larger point: ***Don't use jargon unless you have a clear reason for doing so.***

This

Never use the pronoun "this" unless you are ready to answer the question, "This what?"

Because you should always be able to identify what you're talking about. If you can't, then how will the reader?

Use Verbs

In order to write active and responsible prose (in which actors own their actions), ***let verbs be verbs***. Don't turn them into other parts

JARGON AND JUDGMENT   161

of speech when you can avoid it. For example, let's return to the sentence that ended the section on "It is . . . that" above:

> The transitional quality of crepuscular light **makes it attractive to** painters.

This sentence is improved from its first draft, but we can tighten it even further:

> The transitional quality of crepuscular light **attracts** painters.

Attraction drives the sentence. When we express that idea in the form of a verb, the revised sentence sheds unnecessary words, speeds up, and gains force.

The larger point: *Use active verbs.*

> Not: "It is a representation of," but rather: "It represents."
> Not: "It gives power to," but rather: "It powers."
> Not: "There is a causal relation between malnutrition and sickness," but rather: "Malnutrition causes sickness."

You get the idea.

Active verbs lead to more direct statements. Direct statements form the basis for good academic writing because they're easier to read and understand.

Relatedly: *Avoid weak verbs.*

Active verbs keep your sentences and paragraphs moving. *Center your sentences on the verb(s) they contain wherever possible,* and you'll feel your writing pulse with vigor. Weak verbs stagnate your prose. Think in terms of the action being performed.

For example, "evidence" (and its cousin, "evince") are weak verbs:

> His goal of winning the eating contest was evidenced by his consumption of forty frankfurters and buns during thirty-minute practice sessions five times a week.

Instead, try:

> His consumption of forty frankfurters and buns at a thirty-minute sitting five times each week proved his serious intent to win the eating contest.

Or better still:

> He gorged himself on forty hot dogs and buns in half an hour, five times each week, and so proved his intention to win the eating contest.

The first revision substitutes an active verb ("prove") for a weak one ("evidence"), while the second adds another vivid verb ("gorge"). Notice how, as the verbs dictate the structure of the sentence, each succeeding version gets shorter. Active verbs tighten your prose and make your writing clearer and sharper.

Avoid empty verbs.

Empty verbs suggest action, but surround it with an opaque, blurry cloud. Avoid the following verbs (and others like them), especially in describing your argument, because they don't clarify what work the author or object is doing:

analyzes	studies
represents	registers
confirms	portrays
explores	questions

For example, "Blutarsky studies the behavior of flounder and otters" says almost nothing. What does his study reveal?

These next verbs more clearly suggest the action the author is taking:

suggests that	shows that
makes a case for	demonstrates

illuminates how	argues that
answers	resolves
reconciles	exposes

Finally, *avoid weak forms of the verb "to be."*

Not: "permanent income is a better predictor of life satis-faction than current income,"[24] but rather: "permanent income better predicts . . ."

Not: "it is our contention that many outcomes, including the society–environment relationship, are the product of interrela-tions among these social actors," but rather: "we contend that many outcomes . . . result from . . ."[25]

You get the idea. **Here's a practical tip: skim your paragraphs for instances of the word "is."** You'll never be able to avoid it entirely (nor should you), but a proliferation of the word suggests that you need to inject more activity into your prose.

The takeaway: Active verbs lead to active prose in which you assert yourself. You'll make vital, precise statements that your reader can follow, understand, and assess, so you'll reinforce your partnership with the reader.

That's not only good academic writing. It's also responsible ac-ademic writing—which is the subject of the next and final chapter.

CHAPTER 4

Why We Must

Because We're All in This Together

Whatever we write is for readers, or it's nothing at all.

—**WILLIAM GERMANO**[1]

I spent a week in 2006 making the acquaintance of John D. Mac-Donald. MacDonald, the author of over seventy crime novels, had died two decades earlier, but I got to know him through his archive at the University of Florida. Prominent among his leavings were boxes and boxes of fan mail. It appears that MacDonald answered every fan letter he ever got, including some further exchanges with fans who answered his answers.

We might infer that MacDonald was a nice guy—which seems to have been the case. But the author's generous correspondence habits resulted from more than courtesy. As a professional writer who held an MBA and had started as a businessman, MacDonald understood that his financial support came not so much from his publishers as from the people who bought his books.[2] His cultivation of his readership included friendly correspondence with them.

John D. MacDonald cared for his readers. He cared about entertaining them, and he honored their effort when they reached out to him. Perhaps he felt a personal duty to do this, but he surely identified it as a professional obligation.

All writers have their own version of this professional obligation. Well, not all of them. Diarists can ignore this book and others like it because diarists write for themselves. But writers who want other readers should care for those readers. I've stressed caretaking in these pages because academic writers 1) don't learn its necessity and 2) consequently don't get enough practice at it. I've also stressed it because **taking care of the reader is an academic writer's professional obligation.** In this final chapter I want to extend that idea: **Taking care of academic readers is the** collective **responsibility of all academic writers.** That is, we're all in this together.

When I say "collective," I'm not referring just to academic professionals. Professors have no monopoly on academic knowledge or academic writing. However, their efforts have attracted much disapprobation for quite a while now (decades!). Not surprisingly, that widespread disapproval comes from the same readers whom academic writing treats so indifferently. When academic writers don't respect their readers, they produce writing that is alienating, uncommunicative, and un-useful—and readers don't like it.

It's a bad move to piss off your audience. If you're going to do it, have a good and specific reason. Martin Luther King, Jr. wanted to scorch his opponents when he wrote "Letter from Birmingham Jail." He didn't anger them because he neglected the effort to be clear and understandable but because of what he said to them: he held them to account for the racism of their "moderate" positions on segregation. Plenty of people objected to King's ideas, but none of them appeared to have trouble figuring them out.

If academic writers are to deserve the respect of academic readers, we're going to have to do it not only separately but also together, as a teaching and learning community. Members of that community need to look after each other. In these final pages, I'll talk about the bind we're in, and what a change—both individual and collective—might look like.

Useful Difficulty Revisited

Some of academia's most visible celebrities write difficult prose. I'm thinking of people like the philosophers Judith Butler and Jacques Derrida, anthropologist Elizabeth Povinelli, sociologist Harrison White, and cultural theorist Pierre Bourdieu, to name a few. These intellectuals gained influence because they managed to persuade their readers to parse their writing closely and push hard to discern their ideas. Such success seems to imply that academic writers *should* be difficult. But it's a risky mistake to draw that conclusion.

The late Lauren Berlant, a literary and cultural critic, sought useful difficulty. Reading Berlant is *hard*. In one celebration of Berlant's work, Caleb Smith said that he reads Berlant "as a writer, a sentence-maker whose ideas are inextricable from their composition in carefully arranged sequences of words."[3] Smith's appreciation, backed up by his willingness to study this work in depth and detail, points to Berlant's success in vaulting from the world of academic writing to the world of literary art.

But most academic writers aren't artists. Their brief is different—and it starts with the need to be understood.

Most readers will refuse to labor over the prose of academic writers in the way that Smith and many other readers have labored over Lauren Berlant's. For that reason, it's a daring choice to write the way that Berlant does. For Berlant, the move paid off. For most writers, it will not.

Lauren Berlant is therefore a poor role model for aspiring writers. I don't mean to single Berlant out in this respect, nor to suggest that Berlant is a bad writer. Berlant made a choice about how to write and has legions of devoted readers to show for it. That's successful communication by any reasonable definition— but it's hard to duplicate. So it's a bad bet to try to copy Lauren Berlant.

Too many well-regarded scholars—including some I've quoted in this book—set similarly un-useful examples. Perhaps they compose in a hurry. But no matter why, these intellectuals don't try hard enough to be understandable. Their disregard for their readers' needs makes them into bad writers. That doesn't mean that you shouldn't continue to learn from them. Just don't try to write like them.

Fearful Writing and the Search for the Goldilocks Solution

Academia can be competitive, and many scholars—both students and professionals—fear being challenged. Rather than aiming purposefully for Berlant's variety of studied density and crafted ambiguity, they write indirectly, skirting meaning as though it were too hot to touch, so that understanding becomes elusive and confrontation difficult. Instead of clasping the reader's hand, they let go of it. "Bad jargon" (as I've called it) often marks this tendency.

Most academic writers don't turn cryptic on purpose, or even realize that they're doing it. But academic writing can be a high-stakes enterprise, and anxiety makes writers do strange things.

Try This

"If you don't know how to pronounce a word, say it loud!"

E. B. White recalled this exhortation by his teacher William Strunk. It's good life advice, but I quote it here because it is, by analogy, good writing advice too.

Failure of writerly confidence accounts for many academic writing problems, perhaps a whole culture of them. The reluctance to stand up and proclaim your view—for what is writing if not the assertion of the writer's view?—results in a contradiction in action: the writer tries to declaim and hide at the same time. This may take different forms:

- talking around a subject rather than through it (circling);
- reluctance to state a position;
- bad jargon and other forms of linguistic obscurantism;
- hedging—sometimes even before a statement is made.

One frequent symptom of these ills is an overreliance on the word "seems," as in this instance:

> Because of the frequent bias of historiographical accounts—in particular those from the time following a *malus princeps*, as in the case of Nero—it seems promising to have a look at other contemporary representational media (e.g. public performance, archaeology, epigraphy, numismatics), and thus to allow for an expanded and differentiated view of the emperor's image.

The verb "to seem" communicates ambiguity and uncertainty, with an implication of hidden fact, as in: "Mata seems loyal, but perhaps she's a spy." But a writer's decision about what to explore and argue is not ambiguous. If it's not a good idea to look at Nero's performance, then why do it? If the writer isn't sure it's a good idea, why should the reader spend time on it?

All of these instances reflect gnawing self-doubt about one's legitimacy as a scholar. You may be legit or you may not, but you will never gain respect by shrinking from your task. So push yourself to follow Strunk's advice. If you do, you'll avoid the fearful writing that I describe later in this chapter.

Anxiety also makes writers verbose: It can generate a grinding need to show everything you know. Here's a hyperbolic example, a statement from an imaginary guide to angling that's supported and elaborated in three imaginary footnotes:

Fishing is poor at neap tide.[1, 2, 3]

Notes:

1. The tides are caused by the orbits of celestial bodies, starting with the earth's annual path around the sun. For the originary theory of the heliocentric solar system, see Nicolaus Copernicus, *De Revolutionibus* (1543).

2. For a full discussion of how lunar gravity causes the tides, see Isaac Newton, *Philosophiæ Naturalis Principia Mathematica* (1687). Newton was working from an idea proposed by René Descartes.

3. Neap tides result in calm waters in which fish tend not to bite.

Only the third footnote makes useful sense, and in most contexts even that one would be omitted as unnecessary, or else lifted into the body of the essay. The first two notes display knowledge, all right, but it's knowledge that aggrandizes the writer more than it offers relevant context to the reader, who is presumably interested in fishing, not astronomy.

This example is meant to be funny, but less exaggerated versions of it appear regularly in academic writing whenever the writer is nervous that he won't be seen as enough of an expert. Graduate students make this mistake a lot, for obvious reasons. Because they're not yet officially credentialed experts, they feel obliged to show that they've read everything within a mile of their topic. This paragraph, for example, is a blinking Christmas tree spangled with names and labels:

Globalization is the mantra, the deus ex machina of our times. From marketing gurus to young artists, from rock stars to undergraduate students, from world leaders to urban rioters, from Nobel Prize winners to news speakers "the claim that the world is becoming unified as never before seems to have established a powerful hold" (Rosenberg, 2002:1). The so-called buzzword of the 1990s has also become one of the central thematics for social theory and sociology. Neo-Marxists, functionalists, world-system scholars, communitarianists, Weberians and postmodernists, all are converging on the position 'that globalization is a distinguishing trend of the present moment' (Kellner, 2002: 285). There is by now an accumulation of sociological literature that exposes the vacuity of claims to economic, political or cultural globalization. At the same time, as Geschiere and Meyer (1998: 601) remark, "the more current the notion of globalization becomes, the more it seems to be beset with vagueness and inconsistencies." Embraced with fascination and uneasiness globalization functions as a passe-partout that soaks up everything like a sponge. Now, and to be clear from the beginning, this is a book about globalization. It attempts to come to terms with what globalization is, and how we have to understand it.[4]

My graduate school adviser used to say, "You have to write a book with lots of footnotes so you can write books without footnotes."[5] There's some truth to that, surely. Like professionals in any field, writers really do have to prove themselves, and the amount of proof they need depends on their experience.

Yet if you reference everything you know in an attempt to justify all of your research, your writing will look like Grandma's attic: a jumble of boxes, or a shelf to which things are added but never removed. It will be a display—a cluttered story of your reading rather than a clean story of your argument.

The cliché "murder your darlings" encourages writers to remove excess verbiage during the editing stage. It also applies to research. **You don't have to quote everyone you ever read**—and if you put too much in, you'll get in the way of your own story.

For Example

Andrew Delbanco's *College: What It Was, Is, and Should Be* is an instructive example of writerly restraint. The learning beneath the visible surface is considerable, but the surface remains calm, and the passage through the book is smooth sailing, as in this excerpt:

> Committed as they were to what I have called lateral learning, Puritans nevertheless suspected that too much talk from the laity with too little guidance from the clergy could lead to insolence and heresy—and so they stressed the need to hear from learned lecturers as well as from themselves. In fact, their zeal for sermons became a point of sore dispute in old England, where the state church emphasized the sonic and scenic aspects of public worship—the sound of the organ, the sight of the scarlet-clad priest seen in light refracted through stained glass. For those who took seriously St. Paul's injunction that "faith cometh by hearing" (Romans 10:17), this kind of spectacle was both too little and too much. One reason they emigrated to New England in the first place was their belief that the infusion of grace was likeliest to occur not while a penitent sinner was witnessing the sacraments or even while taking communion, but when he or she was listening to a gospel preacher whose voice could melt the heart.

It takes time and practice to write with restraint. Get feedback from honest readers and allow yourself multiple drafts. And remember the remark that the philosopher Blaise Pascal made about his own writing: "I would have written you a shorter letter but I didn't have the time."

The two tendencies I just described—evasive writing and overexplained, source-heavy writing—share an important quality. They're both involuted. In each case, the writer turns inward instead of outward toward the reader. In both cases, the writer raises a shield against scrutiny by the very reader whose close attention she's supposed to want.

Writers may shield themselves by turning inward for a whole book at a time. Not every academic writer wants to write a book, but scholarly books provide a revealing showcase for a certain kind of academic anxiety. William Germano has compared an academic book—"especially that first academic book"—to a snow globe. The glass walls keep the reader at a safe distance, looking in at a bauble that's meant to be viewed from outside, but not opened and explored.[6]

Germano describes this snow-globe world as "a fully-defended and impregnable space" in which "no questions are asked, or invited." That defensive strategy is deliberate, because reaching the reader is decidedly *not* the goal of a snow-globe book. Instead, "its main purpose is to be admired." From this description, Germano reaches a conclusion both logical and disturbing: that "scholarly books, especially first ones, are a paranoid genre." A book can be paranoid when it reflects the author's worried belief "that someone is always watching, eager to find fault." Instead of inviting response and conversation, the author "take[s] every precaution against criticism."

I've quoted Germano at some length because his powerful metaphor suggests that evasive (and often jargon-laden) arguments and over-sourced ones are really two species of the same thing: what he calls "fearful writing."

Fearful writing wants to be noticed but not scrutinized, admired but not critiqued. It keeps its distance from its audience. This is a kind of bad writing, of course. But what chiefly makes it bad is that it promotes poor relations between author and reader.

Fighting fearful writing requires honesty about your own fears. They're natural. In order to write this book, I've had to present a more personal "I" than I've used in my writing before. To do otherwise would have resulted in a different relation with you, my reader—and not one I wanted. So, I pushed through my own resistance. To fight fear, *cultivate critical self-awareness of your own tendencies as a writer.* In other words, know what you're doing—which is harder than it sounds, and an ongoing process. Then use that awareness to *watch for excess in your performance.* And take the opportunity to revise toward the "just right" Goldilocks solution, a middle way that's neither cryptic nor verbose.

Tip
Beware of the talking paper

Another symptom of fearful writing is the talking paper. Constructions such as "This essay will argue" or "This dissertation asserts" deflect attention from the writer who's actually doing the talking—and the thinking.

Essays and dissertations can't think, and they can't talk. Giving agency to the writing rather than the writer allows the writer to hide behind the page and head for the hills to assume a new identity among the goatherders, where no one will ever recognize you as the author of an argument that people might disagree with.

The alternative: **stand up for your ideas.** Take responsibility for them and argue for them yourself. This is more than a suggestion to say "I" (though it is that). As Strunk says, "If you don't know how to pronounce a word, say it loud!"

The Incredible Shrinking Audience

For most of this book I've focused on the one-to-one relation between writer and reader. That relation begins whenever someone picks up a piece of writing and starts to read. I've stressed the need to recognize and then cultivate that relation directly and without fear. But with the exception of essays assigned in school, most pieces of writing aren't intended for just one reader. Most writers graduate from the classroom and seek an audience of many.

But who should make up that many? Most academic writers want a wide audience for their work, but they also respect boundaries and borders—sometimes too much. These borders usually mark a discipline or field, a specialty or subspecialty. These carved-out areas aren't exactly populous. At this writing, the print run of a typical scholarly book is in the low hundreds. The circulation figures for scholarly journals are comparably low.

These numbers suggest micro-audiences. With that phrase I don't mean to suggest that every academic writer should aim to write for the mythically wide "general public." Not every scholar *wants* to write for the *New York Times* or *Atlantic* anyway—and not every scholar should. It's reasonable that scholarship in some fields will never find a wide and general public, and it's silly to condemn writing because it doesn't appeal to a giant audience. The definition of "successful" academic writing need not and should not be tied to the size of its readership.

But that doesn't mean that we should settle for shrinking audiences of subspecialists either. Many academic writers—too many—tend to write so that fewer readers can reach them, with the result that they reach fewer readers. Academic writers need not seal themselves inside their specialized fields or subfields in this way. The goal is simply this: ***Academic writers should write so that their work may find its full audience of interested readers.*** You needn't try to write a bestseller. Instead, reach for *your* largest potential audience. It will be smaller than Stephen King's, but it might be larger than you think.

If "seek your audience" looks like obvious advice, consider how few academic writers follow it. Recall my example from chapter 1 of the writer who cites "Jameson's postmodern hyperspace" as though any reader would understand the term. The problem doesn't lie with the concept; it lies in the insularity of the reference. That move limits the audience to Jameson readers and warns non-Jameson readers against asking questions. It's an example of fearful writing because it erects barriers to understanding.

Good academic writing should lower those barriers, and also others. It doesn't have to cross *every* boundary, but how about the ones that lie closest? It's more important to reach across nearby borders than it is to count heads in your audience. That's because *if you write to cross boundaries, you'll write more clearly—because you'll be more conscious of your own effort to connect.* So don't shrink back from the marked boundaries of your specialization.

I'm going to offer some specific advice on how to practice border-crossing in academic writing presently. (Spoiler alert: it doesn't mean writing op-eds or adapting your dissertation into a screenplay.) But before I do that, I will pause to consider what insularity—that is, staying within borders—has done to academic writing, and with it the larger academic enterprise.

Politics and Academic Language

The problem is not specialization but balkanization. Specialization organizes thoughts and the thinkers who think them. Balkanization isolates them in needlessly separated spaces. When academic writers split their audience into micro-communities, we can lose sight of the larger enterprise. The academic community, and with it, academic writing, loses its ethic.

Furthermore

The readership for academic writing did not fracture suddenly. The movement toward micro-audiences has been going on for many years. Speaking of the need for an undergraduate core curriculum, Dean Henry Rosovsky of Harvard described the academic world as "a Tower of Babel in which we have lost the possibility of common discourse and shared values." Rosovsky said that in 1976.

The need for an ethic has been with us for a while—and that ethic should start with generous, boundary-crossing writing. Bad things happen when writers lose their ethical awareness of the larger field in which they work.

No one understood that better than George Orwell. He believed that such a loss, by both writers and readers, would lead directly to political corruption. Orwell outlines that collapse in "Politics and the English Language," the most compact guide to clear and precise writing that I know of. (The essay really shook me up when I read it as a college student, and I've assigned it to many students since.)

Orwell warns that loose, sloppy, imprecise writing encourages likewise sloppy thinking—which invites political control by mendacious government leaders. In this climate of lazy imprecision, political writers (who write badly on purpose) corrupt careless, uncritical readers. That corruption takes the form of complacent acceptance of the unacceptable:

> Defenseless villages are bombarded from the air, the inhabitants driven out into the countryside, the cattle machinegunned, the huts set on fire with incendiary bullets: this is called *pacification*. Millions of peasants are robbed of their farms and sent trudging along the roads with no more than they can carry: this is called *transfer of population* or *rectification of frontiers*. People are imprisoned for years without trial, or shot in the back of the neck or sent to die of scurvy in Arctic lumber camps: this is called *elimination of unreliable elements*.[7]

Bland, vague language here sands off the sharp points and allows the reader to swallow disturbing concepts easily. This deliberate imprecision is necessary, Orwell says, "if one wants to name things without calling up mental pictures of them."

The dangers that Orwell warned against have hardly receded since 1946. If anything, they're rising. In today's noisy world of rampant disinformation blaring from social-media echo chambers filled with like-minded people who reinforce rather than challenge each other's views, one might argue that things are worse now.

Orwell sought examples from a wide variety of writing, from academia to the Bible. My scope is narrower than his, and so is my warning. Here is my academic version of Orwell's threat:

When academic writers write badly, they make all academia vulnerable to derision and political attack. Bad academic writing certainly contains enough of the imprecision that so upsets Orwell, but as you surely know by now, I'm most concerned by the way that academic writers so easily abandon their readers. That neglect has specific effects.

Some academic readers don't push back when a writer disrespects them. A graduate student might think, "I'm not getting this, so it must be my fault. I'll just try harder." Or a professional scholar might think, "This isn't very good, but I need to read it for my presentation tomorrow, so onward." That's a version of readerly complacency, even if these readers have limited choices.

But some readers won't accept being told, in effect, "You don't matter." Too much academic writing shows contempt: it implies that "if you don't understand me, you must not be very smart." That makes some readers (or would-be readers) angry—and justifiably so.

Many of these angry readers lie outside the academy. Unlike the graduate student or the professional scholar, they have less investment in the professional academy where academic writing originates. When these readers encounter bad academic writing that disdains connection with them, they are apt to respond in kind. We can hardly blame them if they walk away from our house. What have we done to invite them in?

The result? We are witnessing a slow-motion collapse of academic reputation in U.S. society at large. Bad academic writing invites caricaturists to belittle a wide range of scholarship, often without reading it. It invites legislators to defund colleges and universities and pass laws to erode academics' authority over their own workplace.* (A leading scholar of the Red Scare describes these recent laws as worse than McCarthyism.[8])

Bad academic writing invites parents to suspect the value of the education that colleges offer their children—and, in some cases, withhold their financial support for it. Bad academic writing also undermines academic authority and blunts the influence of hard-won academic expertise in the making of social policy that ought to draw on that expertise.[9] In short, bad academic writing weakens higher education itself: research, teaching, and everything.

These deplorable outcomes arise from collective effort—or lack of it. Working together, we mistreat various reading publics, including our own.

Make no mistake: I am not saying that you should avoid disagreement. By all means, court controversy if your ideas lead you that way. But *if you want to goad your audience, let them be angry at what you say, not at how you say it.* Academic writers don't need to pander to the general public. We just need to identify our audience and write so that they can comprehend what we're saying. (They don't have to agree with what we say, either. Informed disagreement has greater potential for resolution than uninformed and implacable opposition.) *Write to be understood.* That's how we can begin to save ourselves from the academic version of Orwell's scene of collapse.

The General Public? How about the Field Next Door?

All of this brings me back to the need for academic writers to cross nearby boundaries. The effort will help you to be understood. That academia and academic writing should be more public-facing isn't

---

* Bad writing is far from the only cause of politically motivated attacks on academic work. The cooptation of all levels of education by partisan politics is the subject of another book—many of them, actually. My point here is simply that bad writing is an avoidable part of the problem.

exactly a new idea. Many observers (including me) have been calling for it for years. The call for "public writing" has become needlessly disputatious because for some, it has become synonymous with "dumbing down" in a search of a "general reader" who is more phantom than human.

"Public writing" is not synonymous with "general public writing." Facing outward doesn't mean writing everything as though it were going to be submitted to the *New Yorker*. When you think public, in other words, you don't need to imagine your audience as the whole educated world. Instead, I have a more modest suggestion: just ***reach out to the field next door***.

What would it mean to write for readers in an adjacent field along with the ones in your own? Anthropologists might write so that sociologists could understand. Political scientists could make their work reader-friendly for historians. Psychologists could write so that biologists might understand, or literary critics could envision philosophers among their readership.

We might call this practice "generous writing." The conscious effort to reach out perhaps accounts for the friendly tone in this excerpt from a book about social media:

> Over the last few years . . . and during the period of our study, the main growth has been in platforms—not only WhatsApp and WeChat, but also Instagram and Snapchat. These platforms . . . are not especially searchable, persistent or even spreadable, but they do consolidate a trend towards scalable sociality. It is perhaps not surprising that as anthropologists we would favour a definition that focuses upon the topic of sociality, because that is what we study. Other disciplines will see things differently. For example, a recent book on social media from a scholar within communication studies develops an approach based on concepts of connectivity, including sections on YouTube, Wikipedia and Flickr alongside Twitter and Facebook. Different definitions are likely to suit the perspectives of different disciplines.

There is a natural temptation to see things historically, as-suming that technology "evolves" in neat and discrete stages. In this view social media appears to be merely the latest popular use of the internet, especially when in some coun-tries many people believe that Facebook and the internet are synonymous. . . . Rather than being seen as a virtual "other" world, social media stands accused of being embedded in the most mundane toenail painting and lunch-eating aspects of the everyday world.[10]

The writers stay conscious of their readership here, and reach out to welcome readers from nearby fields.

Reaching out to the field next door is a public intellectual move. Not all public intellectuals have the same public, after all. When you write to efface the boundary with an adjacent field and think about the readers who live there, you're being a public intel-lectual. You'll also write better because you'll be thinking more about the needs of different kinds of readers.

If this goal sounds reachable—and it is!—we might ask why so few academic writers reach it. Right now there are even barriers *within* fields (such as economics or sociology) that have proved impregnable, so people in the same larger specialty see themselves as residents of different intellectual lands. We can do better, and it starts with writing better.*

If more of us write to cross the boundaries with the field next door, we can create more intellectual community, more connec-tions, and bigger audiences. We'll also write better when we try to reach our neighbors. Each result will reinforce the other.†

---

* Reading and writing must change together in some cases. The arbiters and taste-makers within a field (course instructors, dissertation advisers, peer reviewers, editors, et al.) may practice too-tight border control. These reading practices enforce the status quo and make it harder for writers to face outward.

† My own unusually capacious field of English offers a good example. Writing to make yourself understood by colleagues who specialize in different periods, genres, national literatures, and also pedagogically centered fields such as Composition and Rhetoric and English Language Learning, is already a kind of general-audience writing.

Note to Teachers

Students are academic writers too, and they also write for all academics. Please don't reward your students for emulating the poor role models that they see around them. Instead, offer them a variety of writing models to choose from, steal from, push back against, and otherwise engage with as fellow craftspeople. It's worth the work.

That, finally, is the ethic that academic writing needs. We should be more generous to our audience, starting with each other. Actually, all of academia needs that ethic. Literary scholar Kathleen Fitzpatrick has called for educators to transform the academic workplace through community and collaboration. "We are all laborers in the same enterprise," she says, and we have to build "a more generous public sphere."[11]

Fitzpatrick's call for "generous thinking" should start with academic writing. Bad academic writing isn't just the business of each individual writer. Like it or not, we represent each other. We're in this together.

Each academic writes for all academics. (And it's not affiliation that defines an academic. If you're doing academic writing, you're an academic in my book. And this is my book.) We are judged by our writing. If we write badly, we'll be judged as bad. But if we write well, we have a better chance of recovering public support. By this measure, it's fair to say that good academic writing can enrich the world. Bad academic writing can pull it down. We should write as though our professional lives depend on it—because they just might.

But most writers in the discipline don't try to venture beyond their subspecialized neighborhood.

A Story to Close

I've written in this book about how writers are usually telling stories—that arguments are stories, and paragraphs are, too. In that spirit, here's a story to end this book.

Not long ago my nephew Daniel sent me a chapter from a book by the feminist theorist bell hooks that had interested him. A recent college graduate, Daniel isn't a professional academic. With the range of his interests, his example shows that academic readers—and academic writers—don't all live in universities.

I started reading the hooks chapter quickly at first, as academic readers will. I was reading out of curiosity and also obligation (to respect my nephew). Then I saw how hooks's argument reflected certain concerns in this book—as Daniel had suspected it might. Like the literate blue whale I brought to life in chapter 1, I started reading her writing with new purpose.

I slowed down when I came to this assertion by hooks:

> [M]y decisions about writing style, about not using conventional academic formats, are political decisions motivated by the desire to be inclusive, to reach as many readers as possible in as many different locations.[12]

Here, hooks conceives her political commitment in terms of her ability to connect with her readers. Feminist theory has rarely been accused of being easy or approachable, but hooks writes clearly and cleanly and honors her purpose. With evident gratification, she talks of how her work has reached wide audiences, including incarcerated African American men.

In one specific example, hooks recalls a conversation about "issues of race, gender, and class" among "a diverse group of black women and men" at "a black-owned restaurant in the South." Afterward, hooks says, one female audience member "grasped both of my hands tightly, firmly, and thanked me for the discussion."[13]

Here, literally, is the clasp of the hand that began this book, now reciprocated. I earlier invoked that clasp as an abstraction, a metaphor to describe how academic writers should think about their connection to academic readers. But I've also said more than once in the preceding chapters that abstractions can rarely stand alone. The abstract needs the concrete (and vice versa) for each to be fully understood.

So, the last word goes to bell hooks and her concrete example of the abstract clasp. In this inspiring moment, the clasp of the hand becomes a real, physical demonstration of what can happen when writers reach out to their readers. In the best of worlds, the readers reach back.

How to Use Artificial Intelligence

Unless you've been living under a rock since 2023, you've witnessed the deluge of commentary about Artificial Intelligence (AI), especially Chat GPT, the "generative" chatbot released by OpenAI. There's already a tendency to criminalize the use of AI. That's appropriate if people are using it to cheat. But not every use of AI is cheating. AI can play a positive role in research and writing—if we let it.

Let's start with an idea I've already mentioned, that *writing is thinking. It's not just a list of thoughts that you already had.* Because writing is thinking, you'll often find yourself changing some of your ideas as you write.

Writing is also a process. Your first draft won't usually be your final one. As a process, writing often involves collaboration. Writers benefit from feedback, whether from peers or teachers. I certainly did while writing this book.

Artificial Intelligence—particularly generative "Language Learning Models" like Chat GPT—can be collaborators of sorts, provided that you recognize their limitations and work within them. You would do this with any collaborator. You might show your work to one colleague because you know she's great on the sentence level, but not at assessing your whole argument. With another colleague, it might be the other way around.

AI likewise has strengths and weaknesses. Language Learning Models are good at generating a lot of basic information about well-known subjects very quickly. They're also adept at summarizing. These can be useful, especially in the early stages of research and writing. But generative AI presents its findings in generic, mediocre prose. If you're reading this book, I hope it's because your aspirations extend beyond mediocrity.

Before I go further, let me acknowledge the AI-spotting problems that have attracted so much public attention. Even in these early days of discursive AI, many people are willing to let second-rate machine-authored prose substitute for their own work. The problems with detection and assessment have already ignited a firestorm of hopes, suggestions, hand-wringing, and apocalyptic warnings. These legitimate concerns require collective problem-solving and adaptation. But they center on dishonest writers, not you.

Using AI doesn't equal "getting away with something." Nor is AI new—the internet has long relied on it. You use it when you do a Google search, for example. And there's no visible line between "my intelligence" and "other intelligence," either. It's an academic truism that no idea exists in an intellectual vacuum. We already use other people's words and ideas when we quote and paraphrase, for instance.

I've suggested in this book that you not quote unless the words of your source are demonstrably better than yours. AI writes credibly, but not with emotion or personal voice. AI is not better than you. If you think it is, then read this book again and practice a lot.

The question, then, is how to use AI to help your writing. It's a powerful tool, and you may find it useful. One professor compares it to "a high-end intern."[1] You may decide to use it to start a writerly brainstorm, or to finish one. Or you may want to compare AI's ideas to your own after you write a draft. These are just a couple of possibilities.

But if you do any of these things, keep these cautions in mind:
ChatGPT and other AI does its best work on subjects that are widely written about. The reason is simple: AI works by scouring informa-

tion pulled from the internet. The more information that's available about a given subject, the more knowledgeable it will be. If you ask for an AI boost on an obscure topic, one of two things will happen: either the AI will come up empty, or it will make shit up. (Yes, it really does that. How very human.[2])

Given that the machine may cheat: *Don't rely on AI to know things instead of knowing them yourself.* AI can lend a helping hand, but it's an artificial intelligence that isn't the same as your intelligence. The educational world is rapidly filling with stories of students who submit AI-written papers containing errors that the students don't catch because they never bothered to learn the material themselves. Those transgressions will receive their just deserts from teachers, or at the Final Judgment. My point is simply that, as a writer, you have to know the stuff you're writing about.

If you rely on AI to do the thinking, you become the curator, not the author, of the writing that results. And without an author, the writing will be bloodless. Flat, affectless writing might be okay for a user's manual for your new air conditioner. But scholarly writing across the disciplines needs sensibility.

Luckily, sensibility is something that humans have plenty of. So keep these cautions in mind, and go ahead and add AI to your toolkit. Just remember: use it to help you, not be you.

ACKNOWLEDGMENTS

In an early rehearsal for his role in *Monty Python's Spamalot*, actor Hank Azaria was complimented for how well he knew his lines. He replied that he had memorized them starting when he was twelve years old, watching and rewatching *Monty Python's Flying Circus*.

I started taking notes for this book at least twenty years ago, but it really began earlier than that. Graduate students in English are socialized to disdain the teaching of writing in favor of high-caste literature courses. I wasn't immune to that lure, but I still enjoyed my writing teaching more than I was supposed to. As a result, when I was an advanced graduate student in the late Eighties, I co-taught a writing workshop for graduate students from other disciplines. The workshop leader, Sue Lonoff, started with a prompt I've not seen before or since: she asked each student in the workshop to recall the most memorable comment that anyone had ever made about their writing.

Most of the students remembered criticisms. So did I. I received mine during a course in Modern British Literature that I took in 1980. The assigned papers were each read by both the professor, Edward Mendelson, and the course grader, a graduate student whose face I never saw because he never appeared behind the lectern, and whose name I have sadly forgotten.

I wrote my first paper about a lesser-known poem by T. S. Eliot, "The Hippopotamus." I was a pretty confident college student by then—in this case, overconfident. I did a perfunctory job on that paper, and received a head-snapping jolt when I got it back. At one point (and I wince to recall this), I had written that the poem "sounded a somber note." Professor Mendelson—with whom

I reconnected decades later, and who remains a friend—drew a picture of a little hippo in the margins with a musical note coming out of its mouth. At the end of the paper, the grader observed that I had "bought clichés wholesale" and was retailing them back to the reader. Why, he asked, should the reader have to pay more for them than I did? I had a few good writing teachers in college, but none of them commented more memorably than that grader. I hope he sees this book, remembers his comment, and reintroduces himself to me.

One of those good teachers was Edward Tayler, who distributed a seven-page "Self-Help Sheet" to his students to help them with their writing. That handout bristled with Tayler's witty sense of certainty. It was a poke in the ribs—in a good way—and it served me well beyond college. When I began teaching writing in graduate school and started preparing my own handouts, I reconnected with Ted and he gave me permission to borrow from the Self-Help Sheet. When I told him, not long before he died, that I was going to write this book, he allowed me to draw on it again, and sent me a later (and longer) version. Only a few of his tips appear in the foregoing pages, but their spirit informs many of mine. Thanks, Ted—I wish you could read this book.

I became a better writer, and a better writing teacher, during the three years I taught in Harvard University's Expository Writing Program. I joined a stable of professional writers there, and their company helped me think like one. Director Richard Marius staffed the program with journalists, novelists, scholars, essayists, and poets, with science writers, political writers, and thriller writers and, luckily for me, a graduate student or two. I'll always remember that workplace and the people in it, among them Sven Birkerts, Bill Corbett, Joe Finder, Felicia Lamport, the aforementioned Sue Lonoff, and Jerry Doolittle. When he learned that I was writing this book, Jerry sent me a trove of writing tips he compiled during his Harvard teaching years, all of them redolent with his tabasco clarity. Some of those tips appear in these pages.

Jerry died while this book was in production, and I miss him. He was a treasure.

This book grew out my teaching, especially of graduate students. I tried out many of this book's ideas on them first, especially in dissertation-writing workshops. A few of those students have generously allowed me to (anonymously) enshrine some of their mistakes and give them longer life than their authors might have wished. I'm grateful.

This book also arose from my writing about graduate students and graduate school in the *Chronicle of Higher Education* and elsewhere. Thanks to my *Chronicle* editors, especially Denise Magner, and many colleagues and collaborators. Rachel Toor and I worked together briefly on a project related to this one. I'm grateful for her insight and for the writerly example she sets.

It takes a village to raise a book, and this one has benefited from the guidance of many people. All good writers are magpies—they stud their nests with the shiny baubles they get from others. For sharing their ideas with me, I thank Ed Cahill, Clare Eby, Eric Eisenstein, Clark FitzSimmons, Michael Goeller, Edward Mendelson, Daniel Osofsky, Carlo Rotella, Leonard Skenazy, Min Song, and David Zimmerman.

More people read the full manuscript of this book than any other I've written. I've benefited enormously from their helpful comments. Thanks to Linda Falkenstein, David Galef, Steve Gump, Robert S. Levine, Bruce Robbins, Arvind Thomas, and David Zimmerman. I'm also grateful to the anonymous readers for Princeton University Press, especially Carlo Rotella, who shed his anonymity and shared many useful—and witty—suggestions.

A. W. Strouse has been the first reader, and first re-reader, of this book. This is the third book that we have collaborated on, and I hope not the last. Allen's creativity and thoughtful teaching inform almost every page here. He's one of the most interesting academic intellectuals I know, and a terrific writer himself—and if you don't believe me, buy his latest book.

My other rewarding collaboration on this project has been with Princeton University Press. My original editor, Peter Dougherty, set the tone when he invited me to think about this book with him from a publisher's point of view—and he proved equally willing, and deeply insightful, when he joined me in thinking about it from the writer's point of view. When Peter stepped away from the press, his successor, the talented Matt Rohal, caught me—and this book—right in stride. Natalie Baan and her production team and my wonderful and wise copyeditor, Katherine Harper, gave the manuscript thoughtful care. Peter, Matt, and the press director, Christie Henry, have made me feel more like a member of an extended family than a new author. I've written for a lot of people at a lot of outfits, but Princeton stands out from among them.

The support I've received starts at home. My in-laws, Norman Osofsky and Carol Falcetti, provided me with a place to write when I really, really needed one. My partner, Debra Osofsky, has lovingly supported my writing for over thirty years now. And our daughter, KC Osofsky, has talent that inspires me.

And then there's my mother, Tobby Cassuto. When I was in primary school my mother started reading some of my essay drafts with me. She would ask me questions, especially about my word choices. I recall particularly how she would challenge my usage— and how irked I felt because she was asking me to think harder than before.

When I got to my teens, I learned that my mother had gotten much of her editorial sensibility from Strunk and White's *The Elements of Style*. She had given me that book years earlier, and when I finally got around to reading it, I recognized her source. My mother taught me to avoid clichés before I learned what the word *cliché* meant. She cut chunks out of my sentences and paragraphs, and she pushed me to explain what I really wanted to say. In the process, she set herself up in my head. "It is rare," E. B. White elsewhere wrote, "to find someone who is both a true friend and a good writer." My mother, who read this book in manuscript twice, has been both. This book is for her.

NOTES

Introduction

1. Edward W. Tayler, "Self-Help Sheet" (privately published). The "Self-Help Sheet" contains rules, lots of them, that Tayler distributed to generations of students. It was one of the formative documents of my own college education, and I am grateful to Professor Tayler for permission to reproduce some of his insights—and tart phrasing—in this book.

2. Simone Weil, letter to Joë Bousquet, April 13, 1942; Simone Pétrement, *Simone Weil: A Life*, tr. Raymond Rosenthal (New York: Pantheon, 1976), 462.

3. As an observer as well as a participant in academia, I will add that these readers are all too often underpaid, and that their workload may affect their attention span and generosity. To put it mildly, there are still a few bugs in the system.

4. Paul Krugman, "A.I. could be a big deal for the economy (and for the deficit, too)," *New York Times*, October 3, 2023, https://static.nytimes.com/email-content/PK_sample.html.

5. Tayler, "Self-Help Sheet." Some scholarly writers may want to shake up norms that they consider outdated—a feminist theorist may want to jar patriarchal language, for instance. Such moves have the best chance to succeed when they show knowledge of the standards they want to dislodge.

6. Hua Hsu, "A Guide to Thesis-Writing That Is a Guide to Life," *New Yorker*, April 6, 2015, https://www.newyorker.com/books/page-turner/a-guide-to-thesis-writing-that-is-a-guide-to-life. I am indebted to an unpublished 2021 essay by Peter Dougherty here.

7. You can find Kimball's "perfect" recipe here: https://www.browneyedbaker.com/cooks-illustrated-perfect-chocolate-chip-cookies/.

8. Peter Dougherty, unpublished essay, 2021.

Chapter 1: The Care and Feeding of the Academic Reader

1. Peter Schjeldahl, "The Art of Dying," *New Yorker*, December 16, 2019, https://www.newyorker.com/magazine/2019/12/23/the-art-of-dying; "Mask of the Critic—Interview with Peter Schjeldahl and Jonathan Santlofer," *Guernica*, January 30, 2006, https://www.guernicamag.com/mask_of_the_critic/.

2. Sally Falk Moore, "The International Production of Authoritative Knowledge: The Case of Drought-Stricken West Africa," *Ethnography* 2, no. 2 (2001): 161–89, at 162.

3. Marleigh Grayer Ryan, "Translating Modern Japanese Literature," *Journal of Japanese Studies* 6, no. 1 (1980): 49–60, at 49. Note, too, the grammatical error that attends the arch statement: "phenomena" is plural.

4. George Lakoff and Mark Johnson, *Metaphors We Live By* (Chicago: University of Chicago Press, 1980).

5. Fred Howard, *Wilbur and Orville: A Biography of the Wright Brothers* (New York: Alfred A. Knopf, 1987), 71; quoted in David McCullough, *The Wright Brothers* (New York: Simon & Schuster, 2015), 67.

6. Wilbur Wright, "Some Aeronautical Experiments," Presented to the Western Society of Engineers, September 18, 1901, https://www.amssolarempire.com/PubDocs /Wright_Some_Aeronautical_Experiments.pdf.

7. Steven H. Strogatz, *Sync: How Order Emerges from Chaos in the Universe, Nature, and Daily Life* (New York: Hachette, 2003), 1.

8. Emily Dickinson, "Because I could not stop for Death," https://www .poetryfoundation.org/poems/47652/because-i-could-not-stop-for-death-479.

9. Robert Birnbaum, "Andrew Delbanco," *Morning News*, February 22, 2006, https://themorningnews.org/article/andrew-delbanco.

10. For practical tips on how to "wander through the stacks" in this way, I recommend Rich Furman and Julie Kinn, *Practical Tips for Publishing Scholarly Articles*, 2nd ed. (New York: Oxford University Press, 2012), chapter 4.

11. E. B. White, Introduction to William Strunk, Jr. and E. B. White, *The Elements of Style* (New York: Macmillan, 1972), xii. My description of *Elements* as the best-ever writing handbook needs a qualification: the honor belongs only to editions published in White's lifetime. Since he died in 1985, the "little book" that he built on his teacher's earlier little book has been amended more than emended, with the result that it's not really little anymore. Recent editions bulge with water weight, and it's no disgrace to White's successors to observe that they have proved less clever and eloquent than Strunk or White.

12. Bruce Blackadar, "Rational C*-Algebras and Nonstable K-Theory," *Rocky Mountain Journal of Mathematics* 20, no. 2 (1990): 285–316, at 289.

13. The sage is Carlo Rotella, whom I cite with thanks.

14. "I stole this from someone; I forget who," writes Min Hyoung Song of this passage. Now I'm stealing it again (with thanks to Song), and making a few emendations in my own version. https://minhyoungsong.com/2014/04/02/some-thoughts-on -academic-writing/.

15. Thanks to Anton Borst for this example.

16. A few of these tips are adapted from Edward Tayler's "Self-Help Sheet." Thanks again, Ted.

17. J. J. Scarisbrick, *Henry VIII* (New Haven, CT: Yale University Press, 1997), 62.

18. Thomas Doherty, *Projections of War: Hollywood, American Culture, and World War II* (New York: Columbia University Press, rev. ed. 1999), 139.

19. Julie R. Posselt, *Equity in Science: Representation, Culture, and the Dynamics of Change in Graduate Education* (Stanford, CA: Stanford University Press, 2020), 112.

20. Will Kaufman, *American Song and Struggle from Columbus to World War II: A Cultural History* (Cambridge, UK: Cambridge University Press, 2022), 370.

21. These conventions are reversed in British English, but it's a rule either way.

Chapter 2: Everything Is a Story

1. It's the narrator himself.

2. Gerald Graff and Cathy Birkenstein, *They Say/I Say: The Moves That Matter in Academic Writing* (New York: W. W. Norton, 2006).

3. For a brief authorized biography of Stephen Wiltshire, see https://www.stephenwiltshire.co.uk/biography. Watch this to view the artist at work: https://www.youtube.com/watch?v=LrgbDXtt4UQ.

4. These articles' authors and the journals in which they appear are, respectively, Antoine Guisan, *Ecological Modelling* (2000); Chris Thomas, *Nature* (2004); Willi Dansgaard, *Nature* (1993); and Nick Rayner, *Journal of Geophysical Research D: Atmospheres* (2003). For their citation frequency, see Robert McSweeney, "Analysis: The most 'cited' climate change papers," *CarbonBrief*, July 8, 2015, https://www.carbonbrief.org/analysis-the-most-cited-climate-change-papers/.

5. M. G. Meekan, et al., *Ecology* (2022).

6. Thomas S. Mullaney and Christopher Rea offer a creative and useful set of instructions for how to do this in *Where Research Begins* (Chicago: University of Chicago Press, 2022).

7. Here and to the end of this chapter, I draw frequently and gratefully on "Structure as Argument," an unpublished presentation by my Fordham University colleague Edward Cahill.

8. Dani Rodrik, *One Economics, Many Recipes: Globalization, Institutions, and Economic Growth* (Princeton, NJ: Princeton University Press, 2007), 86.

9. Walter F. Hatch, *Ghosts in the Neighborhood: Why Japan Is Haunted by Its Past and Germany Is Not* (Ann Arbor: University of Michigan Press, 2023), 27.

10. Thanks to Edward Tayler for this one, which I have lightly adapted.

11. The triangles are the invention of Michael Goeller of Rutgers University. I thank him for his permission to adapt them here.

12. Alison J. Hughes, et al., "Discontinuation of Antiretroviral Therapy among Adults Receiving HIV Care in the United States," *Journal of Acquired Immune Deficiency Syndrome* 66, no. 1 (2014): 80–89.

13. Elizabeth Rankin, "Changing the Hollow Conventions of Academic Writing," *Chronicle of Higher Education*, April 3, 1998: A64. Rankin's essay contains some of the best advice I've seen on how to write a literature review, and I am drawing on it here and later in this section.

14. One writing skill lies in knowing what to borrow. I got this lovely metaphor from David Zimmerman.

15. Helmut Kloos, Andréa Gazzinelli, and Rodrigo Corrêa Oliveira, "Nova União Village, Brazil: The Impact of a New Water Supply," *Waterlines* 19, no. 4 (2001): 15–18, at 18.

16. Charles Darwin, *The Origin of Species* (1859; rpt. London: Penguin Classics, 1985, 459–60).

17. Karin L. Adams, Ammon Langley, and William Brazile, "Noise Exposure and Temporary Hearing Loss of Indoor Hockey Officials," *Journal of Environmental Health* 79, no. 4 (2016): 22–27, at 25.

18. That sage is my colleague Anne Fernald.

19. Zairong Xiang, "Transdualism: Toward a Materio-Discursive Embodiment," *Transgender Studies Quarterly* 5, no. 3 (2018): 425–42.

20. Philip V. Bohlman, "Musicology as a Political Act," *Journal of Musicology* 11, no. 4 (1993): 411–36, 420.

21. Walter E. Little, "Introduction: Globalization and Guatemala's Maya Workers," *Latin American Perspectives* 32, no. 5 (2005): 3–11, 9.

22. Walter Johnson, *Soul by Soul: Life inside the Antebellum Slave Market* (Cambridge, MA: Harvard University Press, 1999), 4.

23. Here I paraphrase the aforementioned sage, Anne Fernald.

24. Richard Marius, *A Writer's Companion* (New York: Alfred A. Knopf, 1985), 60–62, at 60. The concept of transition through repetition of words is another insightful Marius observation.

25. Erving Goffman, *Stigma: Notes on the Management of Spoiled Identity* (New York: Simon & Schuster, 1963), 143.

26. S. Gal, "Language and Political Economy," *Annual Review of Anthropology* 18 (1989): 345–67.

27. Kevin Floyd, *The Reification of Desire: Toward a Queer Marxism* (Minneapolis: University of Minnesota Press, 2009), 121.

28. Kwame Anthony Appiah, *The Ethics of Identity* (Princeton, NJ: Princeton University Press, 2005), 14.

29. Annette Gordon-Reed, *Andrew Johnson: The 17th President, 1865–1869*, The American Presidents (New York: Times Books/Henry Holt, 2011), 9–10.

30. Oly Durose, *Suburban Socialism (or Barbarism)* (London: Repeater, 2022).

31. Arjun Appadurai, *Fear of Small Numbers: An Essay on the Geography of Anger* (Durham, NC: Duke University Press, 2006), 11.

32. Pete Seeger, "So Long, Woody, It's Been Good to Know Ya," foreword to Woody Guthrie, *Bound for Glory* (New York: Plume, 1983 [1943]), viii.

33. Michelle Alexander, *The New Jim Crow: Mass Incarceration in the Age of Colorblindness* (New York: New Press, 2012), 198.

34. Alexander, *New Jim Crow,* 173.

35. Garrison Keillor, *Lake Wobegon Days* (New York: Viking, 1985).

36. This clever example is unpublished before now, as far as I know. I didn't write it, but I don't remember who did. Thank you to whoever shared it with me.

37. Shoshana Zuboff, *The Age of Surveillance Capitalism: The Fight for a Human Future at the New Frontier of Power* (New York: Public Affairs, 2019).

38. Lee Siegel, *Groucho Marx: The Comedy of Existence* (New Haven, CT: Yale University Press, 2015).

39. Like this. Was it worth breaking your momentum to locate and read these words? Now you have to go back and find your place again.

40. Atul Gawande, *Being Mortal: Medicine and What Matters in the End* (New York: Picador, 2014), 203. Except for the sentence I just quoted, I loved this book, not least because it's beautifully written.

41. Even literary study has quantitative scholars now. Patricia Gael, a PhD in English from Pennsylvania State University, used "big data" in her 2014 dissertation, "Poetry, Drama, and Fiction in the London Marketplace, 1737–1749," https://etda .libraries.psu.edu/files/final_submissions/9726. I interviewed Gael in 2015 (Leonard

Cassuto, "The Alt-Ac Job Search: A Case Study," *Chronicle of Higher Education*, December 11, 2015, https://www.chronicle.com/article/the-alt-ac-job-search-a-case-study/).

42. If your writing regularly requires visuals, consult a good book that goes into depth and detail, such as Edward R. Tufte's *The Visual Display of Quantitative Information*, 2nd ed. (Cheshire, CT: Graphics Press, 2001), or Doig Simmonds, ed., *Charts & Graphs: Guidelines for the Visual Presentation of Statistical Data* (Cambridge, MA: MIT Press, 1981).

43. David Byler, "Trump's GOP Foes Are Scared. But Not as Much as They Should Be," *Washington Post*, December 28, 2022, https://www.washingtonpost.com/opinions/2022/12/28/trump-2024-nightmare-scenarios-gop/.

44. Bloomberg, January 5, 2012. https://www.bloomberg.com/news/articles/2012-01-05/why-some-cities-are-healthier-than-others

45. The source of this figure was https://personalfinancedata.com/networth-percentile-calculator/.

Chapter 3: Jargon and Judgment

1. Uta-Renate Blumenthal, *The Investiture Controversy: Church and Monarchy from the Ninth to the Twelfth Century* (Philadelphia: University of Pennsylvania Press, 1988), 1.

2. Ada Ferrer, *Cuba: An American History* (New York: Scribner, 2021), 36.

3. Paul Prior, "Response, Revision, Disciplinarity: A Microhistory of a Dissertation Prospectus in Sociology," *Written Communication* 11 (1994): 483–533.

4. Paraphrase by the estimable A. W. Strouse, who is not a composition scholar (though he has taught the course).

5. Mark Seltzer, *Serial Killers: Death and Life in America's Wound Culture* (New York: Routledge, 1998), 19. I have excised parenthetical citations from this passage.

6. Eric Lott, *Love and Theft: Blackface Minstrelsy and the American Working Class* (1993; rpt. Oxford: Oxford University Press, 2013), 96.

7. Sonia K. Katyal, "Democracy & Distrust in an Era of Artificial Intelligence," *Daedalus* 151, no. 2 (2022): 322–34, at 328.

8. Ester Gimbernat de González, "Speaking through the Voices of Love," in Stephanie Merrim, ed., *Feminist Perspectives on Sor Juana Inés de la Cruz* (Detroit: Wayne State University Press, 1991), 162–76.

9. Tatyana J. Elizarenkova and Wendy Doniger, *Language and the Style of the Vedic Ṛṣis* (SUNY Press, 1995), 289.

10. Kandice Chuh, *Imagine Otherwise: On Asian Americanist Critique* (Durham, NC: Duke University Press, 2003), 51.

11. The World Counts, https://www.theworldcounts.com/challenges/planet-earth/forests-and-deserts/rate-of-deforestation; Jeffrey Kluger, "The Amazon Fires, from an Extraterrestrial Perspective," *Time*, September 6, 2019, https://time.com/5670432/amazon-fires-from-space/.

12. Adam Gopnik, "As Big as the Ritz: The Mythology of the Fitzgeralds," *New Yorker*, September 15, 2014, https://www.newyorker.com/magazine/2014/09/22/big-ritz.

13. Penelope Green, "Marilyn Loden, Who Championed a Feminist Metaphor, Dies at 76," *New York Times*, September 3, 2022, https://www.nytimes.com/2022/09/03/us/marilyn-loden-dead.html.

14. Patricia A. Ybarra, *Latinx Theater in the Times of Neoliberalism* (Evanston, IL: Northwestern University Press, 2018).

15. Malcolm Voyce, *Foucault and Family Relations: Governing from a Distance in Australia* (Lanham, MD: Lexington, 2019), 142.

16. Johnathan Thayer, *City of Workers, City of Struggle: How Labor Movements Changed New York* (New York: Columbia University Press, 2021), 41.

17. See James Fallows, "Mistakes Were Made," *Atlantic Monthly*, February 19, 2015, https://www.theatlantic.com/politics/archive/2015/02/mistakes-were-made/385663/.

18. Laurence Urdang, ed. *The New York Times Everyday Reader's Dictionary of Misunderstood, Misused, Mispronounced Words* (New York: Weathervane, 1972), n.p.

19. Edward Mendelson, unpublished handout.

20. Mary Douglas, *Purity and Danger: An Analysis of Concepts of Pollution and Taboo* (1966; rpt. London: Routledge, 2002), 146.

21. Leonard Cassuto, *Hard-Boiled Sentimentality: The Secret History of American Crime Stories* (New York: Columbia University Press, 2009), 256.

22. Alexander Gregory, Ian Walker, Kevin Mclaughlin, and Adam D. Peets, "Both Preparing to Teach and Teaching Positively Impact Learning Outcomes for Peer Teachers," *Medical Teacher* 33, no. 8 (2011): e417–e422,

23. Yu-Fang Cho, "Rewriting Exile, Remapping Empire, Re-Membering Home: Hualing Nieh's 'Mulberry and Peach,'" *Meridians* 5, no. 1 (2004): 157–200, at 188.

24. Tim Futing Lao, "Income Inequality, Social Comparison, and Happiness in the United States," *Socius* 7 (2021): 1–17, at 2.

25. Dana R. Fisher and Andrew K. Jorgenson, "Ending the Stalemate: Toward a Theory of Anthro-Shift," *Sociological Theory* 37, no. 4 (2019): 342–62, at 345.

Chapter 4: Why We Must

1. William Germano, "Dare We Write for Readers?" *Chronicle of Higher Education*, April 26, 2013: B7.

2. Because of his business background, MacDonald understood the professional side of writing better than most of his peers. He quickly became savvy in his relations with his publisher, and for much of his career he continued to write "paperback originals" (books that did not come out in hardcover) because he could make more money off them, even though publishing in hardcover was and remains more prestigious. Not surprisingly, complex and crooked business plots were one of MacDonald's signatures as a crime writer. His first book appeared in 1950, his last in 1985, the year before he died.

3. Caleb Smith, "The Berlant Opening," In the Moment (blog), July 20, 2021, https://critinq.wordpress.com/2021/07/20/the-berlant-opening/.

4. Dieter Cortvriendt, "The Becoming of a Global World: Technology/Networks/Power/Life," PhD dissertation, Department of Sociology, Catholic University of Leuven, 2007, 9.

5. Alan Heimert (1928–1999).

6. Germano, "Dare We Write for Readers?" Quotations from the next two paragraphs are from the same source.

7. George Orwell, "Politics and the English Language," *Horizon*, April 1946, 261.

8. Ellen Schrecker, "Yes, These Bills Are the New McCarthyism," Academe Blog (blog), September 9, 2021, https://academeblog.org/2021/09/12/yes-these-bills-are -the-new-mccarthyism/. In a decision against one of these laws in Florida, the judge invoked Orwell. Jack Stripling, "Channeling Orwell, Judge Blasts Florida's 'Dystopian' Ban on 'Woke' Instruction," *Chronicle of Higher Education*, November 17, 2022, https:// www.chronicle.com/article/conjuring-orwell-florida-judge-blasts-dystopian-ban-on -woke-instruction.

9. Alan Sokal's successful 1996 hoax of the cultural studies journal *Social Text* is well known. A more recent hoax in the Sokal mold perpetrated by Peter Boghossian and others was more malicious, and reflects the harshness of the conversation around academic writing. It was a scattershot attempt to test the system of peer review—which relies on good-faith actors—and this bad-faith and only partially successful attempt to undermine it amounts to a case of intellectual vandalism. Yascha Mounk, "What an Audacious Hoax Reveals About Academia," *The Atlantic*, October 5, 2018, https://www .theatlantic.com/ideas/archive/2018/10/new-sokal-hoax/572212/. Less violent but also scornful was the *Oxford Review*'s 2017 list of examples of "academic gibberish": "Deciphering Academic Papers—9 Examples of Academic Gibberish," https://oxford-review .com/9-examples-of-academic-nonsense-deciphering-academic-papers/.

10. Daniel Miller, Elisabetta Costa, Nell Haynes, Tom McDonald, Razvan Nicolescu, Jolynna Sinanan, Juliano Spyer, Shriram Venkatraman, and Xinyuan Wang, *How the World Changed Social Media* (London: UCL Press, 2016), 10–11.

11. Kathleen Fitzpatrick, *Generous Thinking: A Radical Approach to Saving the University* (Baltimore: Johns Hopkins University Press, 2019), 235.

12. bell hooks, *Teaching to Transgress* (New York: Routledge, 1994), 71.

13. hooks, *Teaching to Transgress*, 73.

Appendix: How to Use Artificial Intelligence

1. Pranshu Verma and Gerrit De Vynck, "ChatGPT Took Their Jobs. Now They Walk Dogs and Fix Air Conditioners," *Washington Post*, June 2, 2023, https://www .washingtonpost.com/technology/2023/06/02/ai-taking-jobs/.

2. Benjamin Weiser, "Here's What Happens When Your Lawyer Uses ChatGPT," *New York Times*, May 27, 2023, https://www.nytimes.com/2023/05/27/nyregion/avianca -airline-lawsuit-chatgpt.html.

Notes to Text Boxes

The following notes apply to the text boxes. Numbers in parentheses refer to the page on which the box appears.

Introduction

(6) Louis Menand, *The Free World: Art and Thought in the Cold War* (New York: Farrar Straus and Giroux, 2021), 611.

(12) Min Hyoung Song, "Some Thoughts on Academic Writing," April 2, 2014, https://minhyoungsong.com/2014/04/02/some-thoughts-on-academic-writing/.

(12) Mendelson: unpublished handout.

Chapter 1

(33) See https://www.nature.com/scitable/topicpage/scientific-papers-13815490/.

Chapter 2

(57) Lots of writers have expressed this sentiment, including O'Connor, who did not actually use the exact words that are so often credited to her. In a 1948 letter to her publisher, O'Connor said, "I must tell you how I work. I don't have my novel outlined and I have to write to discover what I am doing. . . . I don't know so well what I think until I see what I say; then I have to say it over again." Flannery O'Connor, Letter to Farrar Straus and Giroux, July 21, 1948, in *The Habit of Being: Letters of Flannery O'Connor*, edited by Sally Fitzgerald (New York: Farrar Straus and Giroux, 1979), 5.

(58) John McPhee, "Structure," *New Yorker*, January 6, 2013, https://www.newyorker.com/magazine/2013/01/14/structure.

(63) *"Turn Every Page": Inside the Robert A. Caro Archive*, 2022 exhibition at the New-York Historical Society.

(66) Philippe Bourgois, Laurie Hart, Fernando Montero, and George Karandinos, "The Political and Emotional Economy of Violence in US Inner City Narcotics Markets," in *Ritual, Emotion, Violence: Studies on the Micro-Sociology of Randall Collins*, ed. Elliot Weininger, Annette Lareau, and Omar Lizardo (Abingdon, UK: Routledge, 2018), 46–77. Sarah Schulman, *Gentrification of the Mind: Witness to a Lost Imagination* (Berkeley: University of California Press, 2013).

(67) James C. Scott, *Domination and the Arts of Resistance* (New Haven, CT: Yale University Press, 1990), chapter 1.

(70) Zadie Smith, "Getting In and Out," *Harper's Magazine*, July 2017, 83–89.

(71) Tony Collins, *Sport in Capitalist Society* (London: Routledge, 2013), vii.

(78) R. N. Whybray, "What Do We Know about Ancient Israel?" *Israel's Past in Present Research: Essays on Ancient Israelite Historiography*, edited by V. Philips Long (Winona Lake, IN: Eisenbrauns, 1999), 186.

(78) Camille Parmesan and Gary Yohe, "A Globally Coherent Fingerprint of Climate Change Impacts across Natural Systems," *Nature* 421, no. 6918 (2003): 37–42.

(80) Unpublished handout.

(83) Martin L. Johnson, *Main Street Movies: The History of Local Film in the United States* (Bloomington: Indiana University Press, 2018), 259.

(91) Graduate student paper, author's collection. Letter quotations from Raymond Chandler, *Selected Letters of Raymond Chandler*, edited by Frank McShane (New York: Columbia University Press, 1981), 184.

(98) David Haglund, "Did Hemingway Really Write His Famous Six-Word Story?" *Slate*, January 31, 2013, https://slate.com/culture/2013/01/for-sale-baby-shoes-never-worn-hemingway-probably-did-not-write-the-famous-six-word-story.html.

(105) Stephen Greenblatt, *Marvelous Possessions: The Wonder of the New World* (Chicago: University of Chicago Press, 2017), 103.

Chapter 3

(134) Paul Starr, *The Social Transformation of American Medicine* (New York: Basic Books, 1982), 86.

(138) Brian D. Bethune, "Langston Hughes' Lost Translation of Federico García Lorca's 'Blood Wedding,'" *Langston Hughes Review* 15, no. 1 (1997): 24–36. David Harvey, *A Companion to Marx's "Capital": The Complete Edition* (London: Verso, 2018).

(139) Car: https://www.smithsonianmag.com/smithsonian-institution/these -photos-deconstructed-devices-reveal-their-hidden-beauty-180960316/. Egg roll: https://thehealthyepicurean.com/deconstructed-egg-rolls/.

(149) Lionel Trilling, "On the Death of a Friend," *Commentary* 29 (February 1960), 93, qtd. in Menand, *Free World*, 164.

Chapter 4

(168) Anne Wolsfeld, "How to Portray the Princeps: Visual Imperial Representation from Nero to Domitian," in *Flavian Responses to Nero's Rome*, ed. Mark Heerink and Esther Meijer (Amsterdam: Amsterdam University Press, 2002), 246.

(171) Andrew Delbanco, *College: What It Was, Is, and Should Be* (Princeton, NJ: Princeton University Press, 2023), 61.

(175) Edward B. Fiske, "Harvard Renews Drive for Major Overhaul in Liberal Arts," *New York Times*, November 10, 1976, B4.